"*Why It's OK to Own a Gun* is a model of civil, intelligent, and persuasive discourse on a hot-button issue. It breaks new ground and offers a novel argument for the permissibility of gun ownership that should interest researchers, journalists and the general public. It is a joy to read."

John Thrasher, *Chapman University*

"An excellent book, rigorously argued but sprinkled with personality throughout. A good example of philosophical analysis on a hot-button issue, the book works both as a general introduction to the topic and as an original contribution to the philosophical literature on gun rights/prohibition. Extremely well-written, it discusses sometimes conceptually difficult material with a very light touch."

Dan Waxman, *National University of Singapore*

Why It's OK
to Own a Gun

Why It's OK to Own a Gun explores the right to self-defense, but also looks beyond it to what gun ownership fundamentally means in American life. Guns can provide a source of meaning that doesn't depend on how much money you have or how important your job is. Guns can offer a sense of shared identity that's not hung up on intellectual credentials or ideological orthodoxy. For many responsible gun owners, owning a gun is a way of positively reclaiming one's own agency in the world.

It's true that guns matter to only a minority of Americans, but the same could be said for many important political liberties. Like freedom of religion and freedom of expression, guns should be on the list of basic rights. In fact, they are: as some in America's founding generation anticipated, gun rights have offered a bulwark for republican freedom. Because there is nothing morally wrong with any of these values, owning a gun is OK.

Ryan W. Davis is Associate Professor of Political Science at Brigham Young University. He is interested in how moral disagreements affect relationships and reasoning. Most of his work is connected to the value of autonomy in morality and politics. He has a PhD from Princeton University.

Why It's OK: The Ethics and Aesthetics of How We Live

ABOUT THE SERIES:

Philosophers often build cogent arguments for unpopular positions. Recent examples include cases against marriage and pregnancy, for treating animals as our equals, and dismissing some popular art as aesthetically inferior. What philosophers have done less often is to offer compelling arguments for widespread and established human behavior, like getting married, having children, eating animals, and going to the movies. But if one role for philosophy is to help us reflect on our lives and build sound justifications for our beliefs and actions, it seems odd that philosophers would neglect arguments for the lifestyles most people—including many philosophers—actually lead. Unfortunately, philosophers' inattention to normalcy has meant that the ways of life that define our modern societies have gone largely without defense, even as whole literatures have emerged to condemn them.

Why It's OK: The Ethics and Aesthetics of How We Live seeks to remedy that. It's a series of books that provides accessible, sound, and often new and creative arguments for widespread ethical and aesthetic values. Made up of short volumes that assume no previous knowledge of philosophy from the reader, the series recognizes that philosophy is just as important for understanding what we already believe as it is for criticizing the status quo. The series isn't meant to make us complacent about what we value; rather, it helps and challenges us to think more deeply about the values that give our daily lives meaning.

Titles in Series:

Why It's OK to Want to Be Rich

Jason Brennan

Why It's OK to Be of Two Minds

Jennifer Church

Why It's OK to Ignore Politics

Christopher Freiman

Why It's OK to Make Bad Choices

William Glod

Why It's OK to Enjoy the Work of Immoral Artists

Mary Beth Willard

Why It's OK to Speak Your Mind

Hrishikesh Joshi

Why It's OK to Be a Slacker

Alison Suen

Why It's OK to Eat Meat

Dan C. Shahar

Why It's OK to Love Bad Movies

Matthew Strohl

Why It's OK to Not Be Monogamous

Justin L. Clardy

Why It's OK to Trust Science

Keith M. Parsons

Why It's OK to Be a Sports Fan

Alfred Archer and Jake Wojtowicz

Why It's OK Not to Think for Yourself

Jonathan Matheson

Why It's OK to Own a Gun

Ryan W. Davis

Why It's OK to Own a Gun

RYAN W. DAVIS

Why It's OK
to Own a Gun

Routledge
Taylor & Francis Group

NEW YORK AND LONDON

Designed cover image: Andy Goodman © Taylor & Francis

First published 2024
by Routledge
605 Third Avenue, New York, NY 10158

and by Routledge
4 Park Square, Milton Park, Abingdon, Oxon, OX14 4RN

Routledge is an imprint of the Taylor & Francis Group, an informa business

© 2024 Taylor & Francis

The right of Ryan W. Davis to be identified as author of this work has been
asserted in accordance with sections 77 and 78 of the Copyright, Designs
and Patents Act 1988.

ISBN: 978-0-367-14106-6 (hbk)
ISBN: 978-0-367-14107-3 (pbk)
ISBN: 978-1-003-43481-8 (ebk)

DOI: 10.4324/9781003434818

Typeset in Joanna and Din
by Apex CoVantage, LLC

For my parents, who taught me to keep my head down and both eyes open.

Contents

xii **Contents**

On June 25, 1844, John Solomon Fullmer accompanied Joseph and Hyrum Smith as they travelled from the Mormon settlement of Nauvoo, Illinois to surrender to civil authorities in the nearby town of Carthage. Relations between the Latter-day Saints and their neighbors had deteriorated, culminating in the destruction of a non-Mormon newspaper in Nauvoo on June 10th. Arrest warrants were put out for Joseph and Hyrum. Recalling a history of anti-Mormon violence, the brothers were mistrustful of receiving fair treatment outside their city. With assurances of protection from the governor, they agreed to leave Nauvoo for Carthage.

Fullmer was a friend of the Smiths and a member of the Nauvoo Legion, a state-authorized city militia. After two years of interest in the new faith, he and his family had converted to the Church of Jesus Christ of Latter-day Saints and moved to Illinois to join other members. Anxious for the brothers' safety, Fullmer was one of a handful of legion members to join the Smiths as they travelled to Carthage and awaited trial at the Carthage jail. On June 26, the day after the Smiths had turned themselves in, Joseph sent Fullmer away from town on an errand. Before leaving, Fullmer gave his single-barrel pistol to Joseph. The next day, long simmering political divisions boiled over, and two-hundred men stormed the jail. Joseph and Hyrum each discharged

DOI: 10.4324/9781003434818-1

pistols, including the one left by Fullmer. Seconds later, both brothers were shot and killed.

My purpose in starting with this grim story is to offer three perspectives on it from a moral point of view. The first is that the Smiths' use of the gun was morally bad. They would have been, for example, better Christian martyrs if they had met violence with nonviolence. The second is that their use of guns was morally irrelevant. It achieved nothing or almost nothing. The third perspective is that there is something morally admirable about it. True enough, it achieved nothing, but achieving something isn't the only thing that matters.

This is a book about morality and guns. My aim is to argue that it is ok to own a gun. I am interested in two kinds of claims. The first is a claim about whether there is a moral right to own a gun. I believe that there is. More than that, though, I am interested in a claim about the ethics of gun ownership. That is, I believe not only that there is a moral right to own a gun, but also that owning a gun is a morally acceptable thing to do. Owning a gun can be part of a meaningful life. This may sound trivial enough, but in the contemporary United States, guns are a lightning rod for the culture war. I offer this book as a defense of the normative acceptability of owning guns and using them in responsible ways.

I realize that some proponents of gun control will say they have no quarrel with that claim. I will likely take policy positions that they differ with, but I'm happy to accept fellow travelers as far as they are willing to come along with me. I also want to acknowledge up front that although I will be defending the thesis that it's ok to own a gun, I also endorse the thesis that "It's ok to not own a gun," as well as "It's ok to hate guns." I believe rights to gun ownership should be guaranteed among the suite of liberal rights. But it is equally a part of liberalism that people have the right to dislike guns, gun users, and gun cultures. On these questions, morality is silent. There is nothing better about loving guns than hating them. All morality asks of us is that we respect each other as moral agents. Beyond that, the rest is optional.

One other clarification is needed up front. Although I will be defending polemical claims about gun rights, I understand that no one on the other side is going to be persuaded by them. In fact, I don't even aim at persuading my opponent. Psychology reveals – especially on politically charged topics – that arguments do little in the way of persuasion. My hope instead is just to describe a way of life that my opponent might not be familiar with. I want to describe it in a sympathetic way, calling attention to what I think are its genuinely worthwhile features. Debates about guns are marked not only by disagreement, but also by incomprehension. I suspect that neither side has a very good grasp of what the other cares about. Incomprehension is bad because it can inspire the suspicion that one's opponents are acting in bad faith. If you don't understand what gun rights people care about, it's tempting to think the entire thing is a front – that there is no real value at stake, but rather a mere pretext to drum up political antagonism in a quest for power. I'm not denying that there is bad faith (I think it's probably prevalent on both sides), but I do think there are also genuine values connected to guns. And while I don't think I can persuade my opponent about matters of right, I do think there is a chance we could understand each other better. And I allow that I should – in turn – try to better understand the values of people who *really* don't like guns.

Here is the plan for this book. Chapters 1 and 2 lay out a case for how someone might come to care about owning a gun. For the most part, both sides of the philosophical debate have agreed that the primary value of guns is instrumental. Most centrally: Do people need guns for self-defense? Defenders of gun rights have typically held that guns have a lot of instrumental value. Opponents are skeptical of guns' usefulness. In Chapter 1, I argue that this emphasis obscures the primary way in which guns are valuable to people who care about them. It's true that if you ask people why they care about guns, they will often cite instrumental considerations – centrally safety and security. But I don't think this is the deepest explanation of the value. Guns matter not so much for their usefulness as for the relationships that guns, shooting, and hunting make possible. The value of guns is about shared identity. This is not an instrumental consideration, but neither is it about the intrinsic value of guns. It is better understood as something like the value of a symbol. When John Solomon Fullmer left his gun with his friends, it was very unlikely to do any good (and indeed, it didn't). But whether his action mattered is another question. The fact that my family has kept that story of my great, great, great grandfather alive for nearly two hundred years suggests it mattered at least a little.

In Chapter 2, I argue for two ways in which the symbolic value of guns is morally significant. First, the identities made possible through guns are central to maintaining a whole range of concepts connected to shared activity, meaning, and action. The people who care about guns care about them in virtue of how they bring together a host of relationships, traditions, memories, and practices. People have compared guns to religion, which is actually not a bad place to start. Regardless of their usefulness, guns invoke a whole slew of concepts about how people make plans and share actions together. If you're a guns person, there's no substitute that can do the same work. And this, I suggest, makes sense of the sharp fears triggered by the prospect of criminal restrictions on guns. Guns are important to how a small but real group of people constitute themselves as agents. Gun control is perceived as a threat to their agency, and that perception – I argue – is not crazy. Gun control is a threat to the agency of people who care about guns, because it threatens to undermine the concepts that make action possible.

The identities associated with guns are valuable in a second way as well. They offer a source of self-worth that does not depend on professional success or hierarchy. Left-progressive philosophers have written a great deal about how contemporary work is bad for people: it is often stultifying, boring, and degrading. It places people into adversarial relations. And worst of all, it sends the signal that those at the bottom have less value. And those philosophers are not wrong about any of that. They envision a radically changed work environment. But whatever we make of their argument, such changes will not happen anytime soon. So people need other ways of shoring up an identity through which they understand themselves as having value. And guns provide that. I understand that progressive academics don't like this, but I think they also haven't (for the most part) done enough to understand it.

Chapters 3 and 4 are about rights. Chapter 3 goes over the most famous argument for the right to own a gun. This argument is based on self-defense, articulated most forcefully by Michael Huemer.[1] If we grant that persons have a right to self-defense, then it is wrong to deprive them of the necessary means to exercise that right. Guns are a necessary means to exercise the right to self-defense. So it is wrong for someone to deprive another of a gun. Governments cannot permissibly do things that are wrong, so it is wrong for governments to deprive people of guns. Chapter 4 makes two other arguments about rights. The first is that the right to a gun has comparably strong credentials to a bunch of other liberal rights that philosophers have traditionally esteemed in high regard. Philosophers in the wake of Rawls's *A Theory of Justice* have commonly identified some liberties as "basic," or of deserving of special protection. Of course, philosophers have not put gun rights on that list. But, for everything they say about that list, they should. Second, persons have rights against the criminalization of permissible activities. It's common enough for legal theorists to suppose that if an activity is morally permissible, then it ought not be criminalized. And it is – I argue – very difficult to think that responsible uses of guns are morally impermissible. So using the criminal law to prohibit guns is wrong. This argument is altogether independent of how important it is to use guns. Even if you think the liberty in question is trivial, it is still wrong for the state to remove it.

Chapters 5 and 6 take up the empirical debate about gun rights. Chapter 5 surveys the empirical literature. Here I make some concessions to the proponent of gun control. Some regulatory measures do seem to reduce gun deaths. Waiting periods for gun purchases show some positive results and are also supported by a plausible theory. Violent crimes are often carried out on impulse, so waiting periods can reduce violent acts. Regulations on large capacity magazines are another way deaths might be reduced, though the expected total reductions will be very small. On the other hand, I am skeptical of bans of "assault weapons," which I find to be not especially well supported in the empirical literature. And some permissive measures facilitating gun carry by citizens may help reduce crime.

On the whole, my empirical assessment of gun regulation is mixed. The proponent of gun control could certainly make a case that some forms of regulation may have good utilitarian credentials (although, in my view, much less compelling rights-based credentials). But this case is a far cry from most political proposals to control guns, let alone the expansive prohibitions favored by anti-gun philosophers. In the contemporary United States, the Democratic Party's anti-gun political agenda – with its emphasis on high profile but extremely rare cases – looks more like a program designed to enrage political opponents than reduce the total number of gun deaths. Overall, I find the case for gun control – at least as typically envisioned – is dramatically overestimated by political progressives. To get a sense, recall the progressive credentials of the drug war in the United States in the 1970s and 80s. It was true, then, that drug use was on the rise.[2] It was also true that drug use was associated with meaningful social costs and public health problems. But there is a big gap between identifying a problem and thinking that corrective action is a good idea. That action – in the real world – must be taken by a host of political and law enforcement agencies with their own interests, biases, and agendas. It must take into account the endogenous responses by the social actors who are targeted.

For example, gun control proponents like to point to the success of Australia's gun ban in the 1990s. That is a complicated case in its own right, but let's take for granted that it was a success. Australia's legally required buyback brought in around half a million guns. In America, sales of AR-15s alone are more than double that annually. All told, 20 million guns were sold in America in 2020 alone. And unlike drugs, guns are highly durable. They can be kept for generations and passed informally among families; the sociology of guns in America reveals these practices to be very common. Do gun control proponents have a theory of how they could scale other countries' supply-side restrictions successfully? I am skeptical that they do, and I think that limited state-level prohibitions in America give greater reasons for skepticism. In short, I think that the progressive credentials for gun control are about as good as the progressive credentials for the drug war: a massive, legally enforced prohibition based on a real problem, supported by extraordinary political cachet and remarkably thin evidence. It is surprising that progressives – otherwise well attuned to fears over the carceral state – are so unworried about unanticipated consequences of their proposals for gun policy.

Chapters 7 and 8 consider a neo-republican perspective on the gun debate. Republicans (here I refer to the republican philosophical outlook; no connection to the political party) understand freedom in terms of nondomination. To be unfree is to be dominated, where domination involves the presence of other agents who could arbitrarily interfere with one's actions. Some republicans have held that gun ownership makes us collectively unfree, as it creates the possibility for mutual interference. In Chapter 7, I argue against this view. I hold that mutual ownership of guns does not create the structural conditions sufficient for domination, because mutual ownership is compatible with a variety of ways of controlling arbitrary interference. And in fact, gun owners do not feel dominated by the presence of other gun owners – instead they actively hope that other people will own guns as well. The republican case against guns doesn't square with the sociology of gun ownership.

Chapter 8 turns the tables on the republican argument. I argue that there is actually a republican case in favor of gun ownership. Individuals who own guns can help prevent domination. Of course, this is not to deny that armed citizens can act unjustly. But I hold that there are cases where private arms help control arbitrary interference. Madison thought the presence of private arms in America was a great advantage over other countries, and I think – very surprisingly – that he might actually have been on to something.

Before starting, I would like to thank the Antonin Scalia Law School's Liberty & Law Center for support of my work on gun politics and republicanism (Chapters 7 and 8). Thanks to Jessica Flanigan for suggestions about how best to frame the argument as a whole, particularly with respect to the values associated with gun ownership. Thanks also to Andrew Beck, who gave me the chance to write on this topic for Routledge's series on "Why It's Ok To . . ." Two anonymous referees provided extremely helpful comments and suggestions. Thanks to Bonnie Candland and Timothy McKeon for outstanding research assistance. Finally, thank you to my parents, Jane Davis and Terry Davis.

CONCLUSION

Here is the big picture thought: It's very hard to understand values we do not share. My aim in this book is to reconstruct the values associated with guns. If these values are anywhere near as important as I think they are, then this shows there are multiple bases for a right to personally own a gun. Maybe more important though, it shows there is nothing morally suspect with caring about guns. Owning a gun is ok.

Guns, Concepts, and Meaning I

1

The Value of Shared Identity

A gun is a tool, Marian; no better or no worse than any other tool: an axe, a shovel, or anything.

–Jack Schaefer, *Shane*

The aim of this chapter is to offer an intervention in the philosophical debate over whether there is an individual moral right to own a gun. By "moral right," I mean to set aside issues of legality, constitutionality, and the like. My interest is not in legal or conventional facts, but in the moral claims of persons. In other words, is there a suitably strong moral claim to own a gun, such that individuals have a right to do so?

This chapter will depart from the usual debate about guns in two respects. First, I will not take any official side within this chapter about whether there is a right to own a gun. Rather, my aim will be to suggest that both sides of the debate haven't fully appreciated how guns are significant to gun owners. For this reason, I will argue, neither side has been able to understand the moral reasons gun owners have for wanting a right to own guns. I will be writing from a perspective in deep sympathy with gun rights. But I won't make claims about that for now. So while this will be an entry in the moral philosophical debate about guns, it won't be aimed at persuasion. Instead, it will seek to establish a better understanding of a certain kind of experience of value.

DOI: 10.4324/9781003434818-2

Second, this chapter will indulge in an uncommon amount of first-personal narrative. Besides wanting to tell a story, my motivation is understanding. Psychologists consistently find we understand each other's perspectives better by sharing stories than by giving arguments. So be forewarned, there will be stories ahead!

Here is the agenda. I'll first characterize one argument in the philosophical debate over guns. According to what I'll call the *binary value premise* in this argument, guns can either have intrinsic value, or they can have value for their usefulness in achieving certain legitimate purposes. Some version of this premise is accepted by gun rights proponents and skeptics alike. However, I believe it misunderstands the way in which guns are valued. Sections 2 and 3 will describe the value of guns, and section 4 will export those descriptions of value back into philosophical terminology. With the normative significance of gun ownership thereby revised, section 5 will revisit the binary value premise.

1. THE GUNS DEBATE

Liberty rights are, in the first instance, moral permissions. If I have a liberty right to φ, then there is no moral prohibition against my φ-ing. In politics, asserting a liberty right also ordinarily involves the further idea that it would be wrong to exercise force or coercion to prevent me from φ-ing. The debate about gun rights usually takes this for granted. If there is an individual liberty right to own a gun, then it would be unjust for the state to use force or coercion to prevent individuals from owning guns. When I refer to the debate over individual rights to own a gun, it will be as a shorthand for this claim.

It's commonplace to think that rights of this form must be supported by an interest that the individual has in exercising the right. For there to be a right to own a gun, guns must provide some kind of value to those who care about them. What kind of value could guns have? David DeGrazia suggests two possibilities. Either guns could have intrinsic value, or else they could be valuable for their use in some further purpose in which the gun owner had a legitimate interest. DeGrazia finds it implausible to think that guns could have intrinsic value. As a result, he thinks that putative gun rights must depend on an interest for which they could be useful – physical security, recreational value, or something like that. Because gun rights cannot be based on the intrinsic value of guns, DeGrazia infers that these rights cannot be "basic" or "fundamental" or "irreducible." He writes:

> While claiming that gun ownership rights are basic in this sense is consistent with what we ordinarily mean by "basic"—fundamental rather than derivative —it is completely implausible. There is nothing intrinsically valuable about guns, unless, again, one regards them as objects of aesthetic value, in which case there is no need to be able to fire them . . . If they were useless for shooting people, animals, or targets, they would have no special value *as guns* (as opposed to ornaments or paper weights). Gun proponents are not interested in guns independently of the possibility of firing them. For this reason, we cannot take seriously the claim that their value is irreducible.[1] [italics in original]

When people care about guns, it's because they care about using them for some further purpose. DeGrazia takes this point to be uncontroversial, but also to make trouble for defenders of gun rights. Of course, he allows that some people might care about guns for aesthetic reasons, or (conceivably) merely as paper weights or (more plausibly) ornaments. After all, some people collect guns – often out of appreciation for their historic or aesthetic properties. DeGrazia takes these as instances of valuing guns intrinsically. However, as he notes, one need not have the right to use a gun as a gun to engage in this kind of valuing activity. People could continue to value guns in these ways even if they weren't allowed to fire them. DeGrazia imagines that perhaps guns could still be privately held, though with restrictions on shooting. (Alternatively, one can imagine allowance for guns without firing pins.) So, DeGrazia infers that if guns are valued intrinsically, the interest in guns cannot ground the kind of personal liberty right that gun rights proponents want.

On the other hand, defenders of gun rights might value guns for their usefulness – in hunting, shooting, self-defense, etc. DeGrazia thinks that there is a similar problem for using this interest as a basis for defending a personal right to firearms. If the real interest is not for the gun itself, but instead for some purpose for which the gun might be used, then it seems like an open question whether that interest might be satisfied without a personal right to a gun. If self-defense is what gun owners are worried about, then – DeGrazia wonders – what if we could ensure their security more effectively by restricting guns and providing police protection? If such a policy better protected the values for which people wanted guns in the first place, then it seems like they couldn't complain about it. DeGrazia proposes similar workarounds for recreational uses of guns. For example, documented members of gun clubs might receive special authorization to purchase guns. Or, "a more sensible approach" might facilitate members' use of registered, collectively shared club guns "in private, carefully secured environments without owning them" individually.[2]

The argument works by initially positing what I'll call the binary value premise. Guns must either be intrinsically valuable, or else they must be valuable for their usefulness in achieving other purposes. As the argument is developed, the problem for gun rights proponents is that whichever side of the initial disjunction one accepts, there is insufficient basis for a personal right to own guns – at least the sort that gun owners usually want. Where most of the debate happens concerns whether the interests served by gun rights could equally well be protected in other ways. The real issue, according to this way of seeing the debate, is whether people *really* need guns, or whether there are other tools that might accomplish the same ends. Even proponents of gun rights are happy enough to accept this framing, and merely contend that gun rights are essential instruments to the ends they serve. Here is one conservative columnist, writing in the aftermath of the Sandy Hook shooting: "Like a knife or a bomb, a gun is a tool, and the human who misuses it is the guilty party."[3] Also writing in defense of gun rights, the philosopher Lester Hunt similarly observes, "A gun is a tool, a product of human technology; and like any technological device, it exists to solve problems."[4]

Let's recap. The skeptic's argument proceeds something like as follows:

(1) Guns are either intrinsically valuable, or else they are valuable in virtue of their usefulness for other legitimate purposes.

(2) If guns are intrinsically valuable, then what makes them valuable is not shooting or otherwise using them as guns.

(3) If guns are valuable in virtue of their usefulness for other legitimate purposes, then there are other sufficient means of realizing those purposes.

(4) If the value of guns doesn't require shooting them or can be achieved through other sufficient means, then there is no basis for a personal right to own a gun.

(5) So, there is no basis for a personal right to own a gun.

Most of the debate about this argument focuses on premise 3. What gun rights advocates and opponents disagree about is whether there are other means to the ends gun owners seek – security, recreational value, and the like.

In the rest of this chapter, I will shift attention away from these disputes. The issue that divides gun owners from their opponents centers on (1) – the binary value premise. Against this claim, I will try to show that the most compelling value of guns is not their intrinsic value, or their value as a tool. Thinking that this disjunction exhaustively captures the possibilities is a mistake. It ignores the real-life experiences of gun owners.

2. NORTH DAKOTA

By the time we arrived at the rural North Dakota town where we'd be staying for the next week, the sky was already darkening with an advancing summer rainstorm. Black against the distant rolling pastureland and extending upward till its billowing white sails flattened at their atmospheric limit, the thunderhead appeared much closer than it probably was. My sister Liz, her husband David, and I unpacked at the "Quack Shack" – Hadley and Chad's guest cabin.[5] The cabin prominently featured stuffed ducks of various species, memorials to hunting seasons past. Chad did the taxidermy himself, David told me. Wanting to be a good guest, I gestured to a drake posed as if about to land on the water and commented that I especially loved the coloring on a male Widgeon. "Is that

16 **Why It's OK** to Own a Gun

an American Widgeon?" David asked, eyebrow raised. I responded in the affirmative, providing a gratuitous explanation that while there were Eurasian Widgeons, we'd never expect them this far inland.

From the Quack Shack we walked the two tiny blocks to the café. The only restaurant in town, Hadley and Chad opened for breakfast and lunch, as well as a monthly steak dinner. They had adopted the café after moving to the heart of North Dakota's prairie country in search of some combination of solitude and better hunting. Besides the café, the town's one street had only a hardware shop and a bar/gas station, along with a few houses loosely connecting the town center to surrounding farms.

By the time we arrived the café was closed, but Hadley was still there getting ready for breakfast the next morning. Dan and Chad were expected to arrive before long, Hadley told us. I hadn't seen anyone in the family since their relocation from northern Wisconsin, and I remarked that Dan had grown up since the last time I'd seen him. Hadley commented that it had been a long time. Through her explanation I learned that Dan had transitioned to being a man. She talked about having a transgender son in her family, and she was doing her best to be a supportive and thoughtful parent throughout. All the same, she suggested that she didn't have much experience with how to think about her relationship with Dan. It was taking some time for her to understand.

Before long Chad's large, camouflage-painted diesel pickup truck, "Sno Goose" – so named after its primary quarry – pulled into the café's dirt parking lot. Dan was last to arrive. Briefly coordinating, we left for the evening's fishing trip. He had been friends with Liz and David for a while, so conversation came easily as we looked for walleye and northern pike in a series of prairie pothole lakes. Dan talked about his parents a little, mentioning their plans for the café or summer trips.

After a couple of days of fishing, the four of us were headed back into town. Passing a row of trees lining the edge of an adjacent road, Dan commented that he and his dad were planning to set up a deer stand along that line in the fall. They talked for a few minutes about their plans for deer season, and then about snow goose season in the spring, and duck season in the fall. Plans for the coming hunts sparked a kind of enthusiasm for shared activities present and future. Soon Dan was talking about the new engraved pistol Hadley had won at a Ducks Unlimited raffle dinner, and then we found ourselves at Chad and Hadley's homestead. As I watched my pants in fear of ticks, everyone else pulled their handguns from various compartments and were soon shooting targets against a hillside by the house. They talked about the duck blinds and new decoys for the season. I was introduced to Chad and Hadley's other truck – an old Tacoma painted in white and brown winter camouflage. The "Coyota" provided the seasonal hunting counterpoint to "Sno Goose's" summer camouflage (enabling pursuit of coyote pelts in the winter).

The contrast between this day and the one on which we first arrived was evident. Everyone was talking eagerly about what they were doing together now, and what they'd be doing together in the future. The various Opening Days of season were staggered to provide a kind implicit roadmap through the rest of the year, and into the next.

* * *

Though I feel a better writer would avoid announcing the author's own observed moral of the story, I can't resist the philosopher's impulse to make the conceptual point as clear as possible. This is a story about identity and how it is shared. Dan and his parents had good will toward each other throughout the week. They wanted to affirm each other's standing as members of the same family. Dan wanted to show that even though his life had changed from when he was growing up, he still loved and appreciated them. His parents wanted Dan to know that they supported him and would continue to support him no matter what.

But good will alone is not always enough. It can be difficult to find a shared language, and harder still to find a shared practice, sufficient to express common commitments. Finding the right words is difficult. Sometimes it's hard to distinguish between words that will reassure and words that will offend. What's needed, in such times, is the security of a shared identity. Psychologists think of identity as a kind of shorthand for self-understanding. Although you can look in a mirror to see what you look like, there is no mirror that shows you what kind of person you are. How do your different properties and attributes fit together? What should you do in a situation that you haven't encountered before? Identity is what guides our actions so we don't have to think through every choice we make. When our identities guide us, we act naturally and fluidly. When we have to think manually about each decision as we come to it, acting takes more work and effort.

Identities provide built in ways of understanding oneself in relation to others. They facilitate self-understanding, and so when identity is shared, it provides a tool for understanding how other members of your group think about themselves as well. When you share an identity with someone, you can feel confident that their emotional reactions will be similar to your own, and so you don't have to feel stressed over how they'll respond to some new piece of news. You already know how they'll respond because it will be similar to your own response. Picture the last time you shared a laugh with someone. When a laugh is shared because two people are acting under a common identity, you both start laughing at the same time, in response to the same bit of humor. In the best case of a shared laugh, you and your friend might start laughing at the same precise moment – even if neither of you consciously understands why you're laughing. Sometimes when that happens, the security of seeing another person have the same reaction as you can liberate you to keep laughing.

It's no coincidence, I think, that members of the little group I've described in this section only started speaking in the first-person plural when they – literally – had drawn their firearms. Before the subject of the fall hunt came up, Dan talked about what his parents were doing, and how they were getting on now with their café and their other side projects. Once the hunts were discussed, discussion shifted to what was shared. Where would we put the tree stand? When would we prepare for the snow goose migration? How many birds were we expecting in the fall? Which neighbors did we get along with? Any uncertainties evaporated in the natural dialogue of gun talk.

Guns offered what faith, family, history, and all other central identities could not – at least not on their own. The hunt provided an identity in which all parties shared a personal investment, and were confident of each other's reciprocal investment. Everyone knew how to talk about hunting, and once discussion begins, it can carry on without self-conscious attention. Memories of past hunts reminded everyone that they were part of the same group, and the anticipation of future hunts offered a kind of assurance that mutual membership was stable. In appreciating the impromptu chance to shoot together, everyone was recognized as a member of the same group. This was something we did together, and the doing it together secured the terms of the "we" who shared in it.

* * *

On a sunny June afternoon in North Dakota – while sharing a meal at Kentucky Fried Chicken – David asked Chad to favor us with rendering of "American Widgeon," which, it turned out, was not only a species of duck, but also a song. (It described the pursuit of the duck, sung to the tune of "American Woman".) As it happened, the family had a whole series of songs for the slow mornings when sitting together out in the duck blind. Led by Chad's gravelly falsetto, most of them had – as David described it – a "classic rock" feel. My suggestion here is that coherence of the genre is not the only thing that held them together.

3. GUNS AND THE METAPHYSICS OF VALUE

Philosophers on both sides of the debate are content to think that guns are best understood as having instrumental value – as a kind of tool. Defenders of gun rights are attracted to this view because it emphasizes guns as useful. It also rhetorically pivots away from attributing responsibility of the gun, but instead to the human behind it. In these ways, it appears to favor regulating crime with means other than gun control. But portraying guns this way is a double-edged sword. After all, if guns' primarily have instrumental value, then it is hard to understand how there could be a fundamental right to a gun. If other means could avoid some of the social externalities associated with guns, then the positive case for gun rights would be undermined. So opponents of gun rights have also characterized guns' value as instrumental.

I believe this is a mistake. Guns are not primarily valuable because of their usefulness to other purposes. Their value is not instrumental. Accepting the view that guns are valuable as a means alone is a kind of rhetorical Trojan horse. More importantly, it gets the experience of gun owners (at least rural gun owners) exactly wrong. Guns don't matter instrumentally nearly as much as they matter to who we are as persons. Their value is based in how they represent the identities of those who care about them. This is a kind of symbolic value. For at least some people, guns matter to how they exercise their agency as persons.

* * *

During the 2008 presidential primary season, then Senator Barack Obama gave a talk in which he tried to appreciate the resentment he had seen as a presidential candidate in small town Pennsylvania. He commented that in rural parts of the Midwest, jobs had declined and nothing had come to replace them. Ignored by national politicians and faced with hard times they were powerless to change on their own, Obama wasn't surprised that rural Midwesterners were bitter, and that they "cling to their guns and religion."[6]

President Obama took a fair amount of criticism for the remark. Some interpreted him as demeaning the values of backwards gun-toting religionists. It didn't help that the remark was made at a political fundraiser in San Francisco. But I think the popular reaction misunderstood what the Senator from Illinois was trying to say. Obama was not being dismissive or demeaning. He was trying to understand. And in fact, his intuition was exactly right. Guns and religion are remarkably similar in the lives of those who care about them. Not only are they similar, but they are similar in just the way that Obama imagined. When someone's identity is threatened, what they need is a way of reclaiming it. Reclaiming a threatened identity involves showing you are still able to act in the world.

In his book *History and Presence*, religion scholar Robert Orsi argues that most religion is not transcendent. Religious experiences don't generally transport believers to another realm. They don't always give believers a glimpse of some world besides this one. In a series of cases, Orsi relates how a religious person encounters what he calls a "real presence" or a "holy figure" – an agent that somehow manifests the presence of the divine. It might be a vision of the Virgin Mary or even a bag of dirt from a distant shrine. What these stories have in common is that before the religious encounter, the person's agency was challenged in some way. One is denied a voice by sexist institutions. Another is trying to find a way forward after being assaulted. A third is struggling in a fight against cancer. In all of these cases, the person Orsi focuses on is failed by human institutions. A priest cannot redeem past injustices. Medical professionals offer patronizing instructions. Elite leaders refuse to listen. Individuals can encounter what Orsi calls the "effacement of intersubjective reality." Other persons or institutions fail to recognize them as genuine agents, capable of making choices and working to realize their own ends. Marginalized in one way or another, they risk disappearing from others' point of view.

Being denied recognition by others is a big deal. Orsi argues that it "endangers the identity of human beings." People refuse to engage them as equals in cooperative action. Others continue to look at them, but only see them as victims or damaged or incapable. They don't see agents in control of their own lives. Orsi calls this "a kind of intimate exile."[7] In such conditions, the actions of a holy figure can provide humans with the recognition they need to secure – to themselves and to others – their status as agents. Even if other humans don't appreciate your identity and capacity for acting, holy figures still can. Holy figures can listen, appreciate a person's reasons, and even share actions collaboratively. This is how religion becomes valuable to vulnerable persons. Orsi explains:

> So the arrival of the holy figure did not offer a pathway out of the world, an escape from reality, as some theories of religion have it, or submission to it, but rather a pathway back into the world. The holy figure did not make pain, suffering, and violence endurable; one way or another, humans have to figure out how to endure what befalls them, and they do not necessarily need religion for this. Rather, the holy figure made it possible for those in pain and distress to reenter their own lives.[8]

What does all this have to do with guns? Rural Midwesterners whom Obama met in Pennsylvania faced threats to their identity. What kind of citizen are you, if you can't pull yourself up to success? If the American dream is persistently elusive to you, even as you see it being realized by others?[9] What does this mean for your American identity, or for that matter, for your identity as a member of a family or a community – or even just your identity as a person? The citizens whom Obama worried were becoming bitter and resentful might well be described as suffering from an intimate exile in their own country.

Religion is one pathway out of this exile. It is not the only way. This is the lesson of the remarkable achievement won by Dan and his family together. Sometimes religion can furnish resources for exercising agency, and thereby achieving recognition by other persons. But sometimes religion instead offers a focal point of dissonance – a place where different members' identities conflict. What can be done, then?

Dan might have become isolated as an agent. His friends and family might have become uncertain about how to speak to him about his identity. That can make it difficult to talk to someone about their past, as well as to form plans with them in the future. If you can't talk with someone about how they've changed as an agent from the past to the present, or share actions with them in the future, then you're in danger of only being able to look at them, rather than act with them. Dan and his family might have been in danger of living in intimate exile from each other. Fortunately, they shared another basis of common identity. Dan and his parents had a long history of hunting and shooting together. It provided a set of shared memories that held a common significance, which all of them understood in the same way. It facilitated a natural set of shared plans in the future, as well as a shared vocabulary to engage collaboratively on affirming, anticipating, and refining those plans. It provided a path back to community events, a shared stock of jokes and narratives, and a reminder of common adversaries. Guns provided a framework for sharing agency. Whatever their differences, they shared something important.

I can imagine a listener accepting this story, but insisting that the role of guns was mere happenstance. Couldn't something else have secured the needed sense of shared identity? Maybe, but maybe not. Hunting is distinctive in two morally significant ways: it helps ensure the equal status of each hunter; and it sustains morally significant traditions.

First, hunting promotes equal status. Relationships can matter a great deal to sharing an action together.[10] To get the idea, imagine planning a trip with your friends or family members. What's important to everyone is going on the trip together, so it really matters that no one backs out at the last second. Now imagine that you had to make these plans without any shared promises. For some reason – just suppose – promising was impossible. With no promises, you might worry that your friend would get a better offer, and so leave you in the last moment. Promising plays a special role in planning together. It gives each person a sense of security that everyone else will follow through. Otherwise, some people might be more vulnerable to being left in the lurch, and other people might be less vulnerable. By taking other options off the table for everyone, promises provide each person the same security about what everyone else will do. In this way, Seanna Shiffrin explains, they help create the conditions in which all parties to the promise have an *equal standing*.[11]

Not all activities do this. When you go to work, you answer to your boss, but your boss doesn't answer to you. Inequality is baked into the structure of employment. So even if you like your job (which, I have it on some authority, many folks in rural North Dakota do not), your job can't give you a sense of your equality with others. Many religions teach that we're equal, and as Orsi found, religious experiences can provide opportunities for people to re-enter the world of acting agents. But religion also reveals divisions in education, status, and power. Jesus insisted to his disciples that there was no answer to their question about which of them was the greatest in the Kingdom of God. The trouble is that that kingdom is not of this world. In the meanwhile, there are all too many indicators of who's greater and who's not.

The hunt is a paradigm of an activity that shores up equal standing. Everyone in the family participates because they choose to – not because they are forced to by need or exigency. The events are planned long in advance, and each participant's contributions are needed for the success of all. Each component of a hunt requires shared agency and divided responsibilities. If I'm charged with working the duck calls, I can't also be holding a shotgun. Shared plans are held together by shared commitment, and so – as Shiffrin's account would imply – offer assurance of the equal standing of each person involved.

Second, guns are at the center of all of the most important traditions for many of those families who care about them. Tradition, according to Samuel Scheffler, provides the best solution available to a common problem. The problem has to do with time, and the impossibility of returning to times in the past.[12] It is easy, Scheffler thinks, to feel alienated from the past, and from one's past self. Traditions establish similar events to occur at the same time, in the same way, every year. Although it is impossible to go back to bygone times, traditions create a kind of second best. They provide a way of accessing the same feelings experienced in the past, and re-affirming the relationships developed at an earlier stage of life. In this way, traditions provide a home in time analogous to the home one has in space. Going home always has a special feeling. Home is a place where the sights, sounds, and smells offer a sense of security in a transient world. Traditions, on Scheffler's proposal, provide a home in time.

For families like Dan's, the seasonal calendar is marked by days hunting in the field. Traditions involve holidays, religious events, and school calendars – but nothing more centrally anchors a hunter's sense of tradition than opening days of season. Hunts provide a focal point for expectations of the future and memories about the past. Without guns, some people would find themselves homeless in time.

I realize this is just one story, but I want to underscore how thoroughly typical it is. Guns are valued for their symbolic meaning – particularly by people who experience economic hard times.[13] People connect guns to their core identities, and often play a role in maintaining those identities successfully.[14] Guns are broadly associated with individualist values.[15] It's important here to recognize that some scholars in the realm of gun policy have started to appreciate the exceptional place of guns within a specific demographic of people. "The intention and the spirit of the gun policy may be noble and inevitably good, but if there are cultural rights and freedoms which may have been unintentionally transgressed by the policy the result would still be contestation and collision of competing interests."[16] Sociological work reveals the strength of cultural ties to guns – particularly in rural areas. As one respondent observed about the challenges of enforcing gun policies: "People will bury their guns before they surrender them."[17]

I should readily admit that my philosophical story is going beyond this research. I'm offering a kind of rational reconstruction of the value of guns. I think my account is broadly convergent with the sociology, but I acknowledge that the generalizability of my claims is an empirical question. I mean to be raising, rather than settling, that question in this chapter and the next.

4. THE GUNS DEBATE, REVISITED

For the sake of the argument, let's take the foregoing sociology for granted. We're now in a position to revisit the philosophical argument with which this chapter began. Recall premise (1):

Guns are either intrinsically valuable, or else they are valuable in virtue of their usefulness for other legitimate purposes.

Recall the case for this premise was that guns must either be valued because of their usefulness in shooting "people, animals, or targets," or else they must be intrinsically valuable – that is, valuable in themselves, not in virtue of any particular usefulness as a tool. The premise was plausible because these seemed like the only options. But once we accept this premise, it undermines the fundamental right to own guns. If we accept that guns are only valuable because they are useful, then it might turn out that there is some other alternative that works just as well. In that case, there would be no case for a right to guns in *particular*. If guns are valuable in themselves (just as "an ornament or paper weight"), then they don't need firing pins, and so the case for a right to own guns-that-can-actually-be-used is undermined.

How does this argument fare? I believe the argument fails, because premise (1) is false. It is not the case that guns are either intrinsically valuable or else valuable in virtue of their usefulness. Rather, I believe, they are valuable in virtue of their relationship to a certain valuable way of life. This is different from either intrinsic value or value-as-usefulness (what philosophers often call "instrumental value").

Consider, for example, a wedding ring. You might value your wedding ring, but it is not true that you value it intrinsically. In isolation of anything else, the wedding ring is just a band of metal. It may have some value as such, but it is not centrally valuable to you because of what it is independent of anything else. However, the wedding ring is also not especially useful. It isn't as though you need it in order to cut a pane of glass or to spin on a desktop. The value of the ring is in its connection to your own history. The fact that the ring has come to symbolize something in your life is what confers value on it.[18] It is not instrumentally valuable, but neither is it valuable in isolation of anything else – as that would exclude your own history with and memories of it. Philosophers describe this kind of value as extrinsic.[19] You value the wedding ring for itself, in virtue of its relationships (to you, to your spouse, to your shared history) rather than in virtue of its intrinsic properties (weight, reflectiveness, etc.).

Likewise, I believe guns have an extrinsic value in the lives of most gun owners. Unlike the wedding ring, they do have an instrumental value. But focusing on their usefulness – at providing safety or dinner or both – hardly captures what matters about the liberty to own guns. Rather, guns make possible a certain kind of relationship that matters a great deal, and they serve as a symbolic marker and reminder of that relationship.

I don't mean to be insisting on any major conceptual point, here. If you would rather call this value its own kind of usefulness, that's fine. Then premise (1) can still turn out to be true, if in a somewhat tendentious way. But then there will be trouble for a different part of the argument. Recall premise (3):

> If guns are valuable in virtue of their usefulness for other legitimate purposes, then there are other sufficient means of realizing those purposes.

This premise seemed plausible when we were restricting the uses of guns to purely instrumental ones: defending oneself against attack, securing one's property, and so on. However, if guns play an important role in constituting, maintaining, and symbolizing a valuable human relationship, then whether there are equally sufficient ways of achieving that value depends a great deal on *how the meaning of that very specific kind of relationship is realized*. This means that to assess premise (3), we will need nothing less than a complete sociology of how guns figure into human relationships. Of course, I haven't provided that here, but I hope to have offered some reason to think that the more you look at this kind of relationship, the clearer it will be why guns matter so much to it. My guess is the more we know about the group in question, the more obviously false (3) will look.

Imagine, finally, going to study a group of people you've never interacted with before. You discover they have some religious practice that makes no sense to you, but of which they give every indication of caring about a great deal. The best thing to believe – at least at first – is that there must be some good reason why it matters so much to them, even if you don't know that reason, yourself. I'm inviting you to take on an anthropologist's view of the gun owner. You may not know why guns matter so much within that group of people who care about them. Indeed, it may make no sense to you at all. And surface level interactions with members of the group may reinforce your stereotypes – which by the way is a common feature of limited engagement with groups we don't know well but about whom we have stereotyping beliefs.[20] Giving in to stereotype is a mistake. The best interpretive posture is to believe that you don't know everything. They probably have a good reason for caring about their values. If they care about guns, they probably have good reasons for caring about guns.

5.   CONCLUSION

There's one thing that defenders and opponents of gun rights have agreed about: A gun is a tool. Its value is in its instrumental usefulness. Do guns provide for self-defense? Do they enable recreation? Etc. I disagree. I think that as long as we understand the value of guns as primarily instrumental, we won't succeed at making sense of why some people care so much about them. Guns don't matter because of their usefulness. Guns matter because of the relationships tied together by them. The value of guns is about shared identity. Shooting and hunting provide a shared scheme of language, shared values, and shared plans and intentions – as well as ways of expressing publicly that they're shared. As a philosophical matter, this means that a premise in the case against gun rights – what I've called the binary value premise – is false. That premise was false because guns do not matter either instrumentally or intrinsically, but rather extrinsically. They matter in virtue of their relation to the person who values them. Seeing the falsity of that premise opens up a question: How exactly are guns related to the agency of the person who values them? I take this question up in the next chapter.

Guns, Concepts, and Meaning II

2

The Prospect of Conceptual Devastation

What is the relationship between guns and agency in the life of the gun owner? Defenders and skeptics alike talk about guns as either instrumental or recreational. The last chapter took exception to the idea that guns either had to be valued either instrumentally or intrinsically. That view, I suggested, was a double misunderstanding. It was wrong about value theory in general and wrong about the value of guns in particular.

This chapter will continue my criticism of what I called the binary value premise. I will try to show that it's a mistake to think of guns as merely providing a valued form of recreation to the gun owner, in somewhat the same way that it's a mistake to think of church as a form of recreation for the believer. Although religious participation does offer a valuable respite from other responsibilities, understanding religious life as a mode of diversion misses its normative significance. In the same way, I will say that trying to understand gun-based activities as recreation or diversion misses the mark on how they matter. Guns are not important because of the specific activities they make possible. Guns are important because they help to make agency possible in the first place. This claim may sound absurd, but I hope to make it more plausible in this chapter. To be clear, this claim obviously doesn't apply to everyone. But in the lives of a very particular kind of person, guns

DOI: 10.4324/9781003434818-3

help make it possible to act as an agent. And acting as an agent is a morally important thing to do.

1. ARIZONA

My father always wanted to be a naturalist. When we were growing up, he would tell my siblings and me stories about how he had raised hawks and falcons when he was a boy. A few times he was even tempted to bring home a baby hawk for us to raise. He never did; the dirt road we lived on was still "too close to town" for hawk-raising.

When I was young, Dad would sometimes tell the story of how he gave up his aspiration. At school there was a wall of posted job openings. Once in a while there would be a Fish and Game or Forest Service opening, but there were always a host of applicants for every position. In contrast, sales jobs were abundant. He decided to become a salesman, and he hated it every day.

My parents moved to Arizona when I was in kindergarten. They had lived in my father's native Idaho, but Idaho's western cities were growing, and the publicly accessible hunting was drying up. (That's right, they left *Idaho* because there were too many people.) My mother's grandfather had built a cabin in Wisconsin's North Woods, where her own progenitors grew up hunting for grouse and deer. No one on either side of the family had any connection to Arizona, but my parents had a vision of a better land. It was a vision of quail habitat. Having abandoned worldly success early on, they were free to live wherever they wanted. Their selection was the outskirts of a rural town on the outskirts of Arizona's Ponderosa forest. That location – the reasoning went – would offer the best location for day trips to hunt each of the state's three separate species of quail.

As a young child, I became dimly aware that my dad was out of work. One day, Dad came home from a meeting at a soda bottling plant outside of Phoenix. (He had been a salesman for soft drink companies in the past.) It was the rare day of spring rain in the desert, and he unthinkingly had put on his only jacket – a blue raincoat. Unfortunately, his appointment that day was a Coca Cola production plant, and the manager there was incensed that someone would enter the premises wearing Pepsi colors. He grabbed my dad by the collar and forced him from the premises. I recall in my dad's story that he was genuinely surprised to be physically thrown out. Alone outside the building, Dad stood in silence. In the distance, he heard the gathering call of a Gambel's Quail. He looked around, taking in the location. Quail lived here. Good to know.

2. THE POSSIBILITY OF CONCEPTUAL DEVASTATION

This section will set out a piece of philosophical terminology – with the promise that it will be important to elaborating the chapter's central claim. In his beautifully written book, *Radical Hope*, Jonathan Lear tells the story of Plenty Coups, a Crow chief. Plenty Coups's long life began in a dangerous period of conflict with the Sioux for control of the upper Yellowstone, spanned both alliance and conflict with the US federal government, and ended – still on the Crow's ancestral land – in 1932. Lear's interest in the chief was sparked by reading a passage in his biography, in which Plenty Coups describes to his biographer the end of his people's way of life:

Plenty Coups refused to speak of his life after the passing of the buffalo, so that his story seems to have been broken off, leaving many years unaccounted for. "I have not told you half of what happened when I was young," he said, when urged to go on. "I can think back and tell you much more of war and horse-stealing. But when the buffalo went away the hearts of my people fell to the ground, and they could not lift them up again. After this nothing happened."[1]

Lear wants to understand what Plenty Coups might have meant. In an obvious sense, of course, Plenty Coups's life continued for decades after the near eradication of the buffalo from the Great Plains. Further, his biography attests to several events – some very significant – that transpired in his life after that time. So what could he have meant in saying that "nothing happened" after the buffalo?

We cannot know what Plenty Coups actually had in mind. Lear acknowledges as much, but tries to think about what he might have meant. He interprets the chief's words in light of how actions gained meaning among the Crow. A relatively small nation beset on all sides by more numerous, hostile peoples, the Crow lived in a precarious balance. Their need to maintain their land against dangerous foes required a continual willingness to sacrifice for the tribe. As such, the tribe's activities centered around fighting and hunting. According to Lear, the most important actions for the crow involved planting a coup stick, demarcating a line before which the Crow warrior would die rather than retreat. The coup stick signaled that the Crow were still a force to be reckoned with in the world. They held a physical space, whose boundaries could not be violated without confronting a mortal threat. The coup stick gave expression to the reality of the Crow nation.

The other centrally important activity for the Crow was hunting. A flourishing life consisted in hunting buffalo. Customs, rituals, preparations, education, and celebrations all centered on the hunt. Status and honor were conferred for success in hunting.[2] In an unstable region with shifting power dynamics, hunting and fighting were, themselves, intertwined. The Crow sun dance – a ritual prayer for revenge – commemorated past successes and anticipated future ones. The primacy of hunting and fighting filled other activities with meaning. They prepared meals for the sake of a battle or a hunt. They told and retold stories. They saw visions. With the stories and the visions, they deliberated about how to secure the tribe's prosperity in war and in hunting. As Lear reports, "everything in tribal life was organized around hunting and war."[3] Whatever one's individual role, each member of the tribe found success through their contribution to hunting or battle. Their intentions and hopes, wondering and desiring, all took their meaning from these core activities.[4]

The end of the buffalo transformed these actions. With the buffalo gone, life on the plains ceased to have the meaning it previously held. This is not a metaphor – just a description of the reality. Without buffalo to hunt or other tribes to fight for land on which to live and hunt, the core actions became impossible to perform. What would it mean to plant a coup stick, if there was no land behind it being protected? What would it mean to perform a sun dance, if there was neither hunt nor battle for which to prepare? These actions could not mean what they had previously meant. A tribal member could still put a coup stick in the ground, but it would not be planting a coup stick. It might be an act of nostalgia – remembering when coup sticks were planted. Or it might be an expression of a longing or desire for a return to a life in which coup sticks could be planted. But it would not be planting a coup stick, because it would not have the meaning that such an action carried. And in that sense, the coup stick, along with the hunt and the sun dance, would be lost as concepts. When a people lose concepts that structure life and social relations in such a pervasive way, they suffer what Lear calls "conceptual devastation." He writes:

> We do not grasp the devastation that the Crow endured so long as we think that the issue is who gets to tell the story. For the problem goes deeper than competing narratives. The issue is that the Crow have lost the concepts with which they would construct a narrative. This is a real loss, not just one that is described from a certain point of view. It is the real loss of a point of view . . . For an act is not constituted merely by the physical movements of the actor: it gains its identity via its location in the conceptual world. And it is the world which has broken down.[5]

With this understanding, Lear thinks we're now in position to make better sense of what Plenty Coups meant when he said that after the buffalo, "nothing happened." Happenings require action, and actions are conceptually laden. An action is constituted not only by some physical movement, but by that movement being performed in context of a certain, socially understood meaning. If the concepts needed to understand and interpret actions are lost, then those actions become unavailable. And if the actions that become unavailable are central or core actions – that is, if they form the center of a nexus through which all other actions gain their meaning – then the possibility of action in general is threatened. For Plenty Coups and the Crow – at least as Lear imagines them – action became impossible once the buffalo were gone. Without the concepts needed to act, nothing happened.

3. GUNS AND ACTIONS

I believe Lear's narrative raises an important normative worry. Although the case he recounts is singular, the loss of concepts remains something people worry about – though perhaps not usually explicitly. You might be wondering how all this applies to guns. I think it does, although I should start by clarifying that there is absolutely no comparison between what happened to the Crow and the comparatively trivial obstacles faced by any side of the culture war in contemporary America. As I've talked about, America is more polarized than ever. The social science is clear: polarization is about not liking those on the other side much more than it's about liking people on our side. When we have differences with those on the other side, it's easy to forget that our shared rights and liberties far exceed those we contest. It's important for us – and here I have in mind gun owners like myself – to remember that whatever our complaints with our political adversaries, rural Americans' way of life is well intact. Gun owners are not threatened as much as other vulnerable groups today, and our political risks cannot even be measured on the scale against the wrongs and injustices that figure significantly in our shared history.

With these morally serious caveats in mind, I think that Lear's idea of conceptual devastation offers a helpful lens in understanding how threats to a way of life come to take on an outsized moral significance. I want to think about how guns – and the activities around them – inform the concepts gun users deploy in their day-to-day actions. My hypothesis is that guns make possible the core activities through which a host of other actions become possible, let alone meaningful. Some people will not be sympathetic to my arguments favoring the legal accessibility of guns. But I hope that even opponents and skeptics will be able to appreciate that guns matter. Guns don't just feature prominently in the recreational life of the gun owner. Guns are part of how people act in the world with each other.

Here again I'm going to take the liberty of talking about my own experience – although my aim in doing so will just be to make the point as vividly as possible. Asking the reader's indulgence for a moment, I understand that it will be up to me to show you that my own experiences are typical. Later I'll return to rural American sociology to show that guns matter quite generally in the same way.

* * *

The popularity of hunting has been waning for a long time in the American west. Well-known cultural rifts divide regions of the country. You can live a life without even encountering a hunter. But for the part of the country within this admittedly narrow demographic group, nothing else matters in quite the same way.

Many pictures in my family from when my mom was younger involve her holding Bobo, her 12-gauge Winchester side-by-side shotgun. In a well-known family story, she was once going to meet my dad to go chukar hunting in Southwestern Idaho's expansive ruggedly mountainous grasslands. On her way up to the designated meeting spot, a covey of chukars walked across the road in front of her. When my father arrived a couple of hours later, he discovered her Green Chevy Vega in the middle of the road, driver and passenger doors wide open – with no sign of the driver to be found. My mother had collected her shotgun from the backseat and taken pursuit. One always plans to return in just a few minutes. But once the chase begins, there's no good moment to call it off. It always feels like another twenty yards could repay all of one's efforts so far.

Time has forgotten whether Mom succeeded in her quest. The next part of the story begins when my parents – now reunited – finally returned to her car left in the middle of the road. A local rancher had taken exception to the parking spot, and had deflated all four of her tires. My parents had no choice but to walk to the nearest ranch house in search of assistance. Penitently, they knocked on the door. As expected, they received some sharp criticism for leaving a car in the middle of a road used by working ranchers. Less expected, the rancher seemed unable to sustain the hard feelings. He quickly shifted from anger to puzzlement. What kind of young couple could be united in having shotguns in the backseats of their cars – just in case a few gamebirds should venture across the road? They ended up not only having their car tires reinflated, but they were even invited to return and hunt on the rancher's private land.

In one sense, what brought the people in this story together was how peculiar they were. The rancher saw he wasn't dealing with ordinary trespassers. They connected with an easy empathy for each other's experiences. Hunters understand how the pursuit can command all of one's attention. For those who haven't experienced it, it is hard to comprehend the chaos of a chuker or pheasant or grouse taking flight. Such events are rare. They can break hours or even days of monotony. Silence fills almost all of that time. Fall is a quiet time on the prairie. Besides the nearly constant wind through Russian olive trees, the only sound for hours might be the rhythmic crunch of grass underfoot. The fall plains' visual pallet is similarly austere. From the blue grey of the sage sea to the dull shades of brown, tan, rust and yellow among grasses and crop stubble, autumn's subtlety belies its beauty.

The flush of a pheasant contrasts with the entire world leading up to that event. The pheasant appears as if from nowhere, only becoming visible once its flight arc is towering into the blue fall sky. It flashes colors of otherworldly brilliance. A rooster's chest fades from orange to crimson to a deep red hue. An intricate latticework of blacks, turquoise blues and bright greens extend across its back and down to its tail, the bird's dominant visual feature. The tail of a pheasant can be more than two feet in length, making the chicken sized bird look absurdly large in the air. Once in flight, the pheasant's wings beat with such sudden violence that they're felt as much as heard, the sound obscured partly by the bird's boisterous crowing as it gains altitude. There is nothing about the tranquil fall setting from which it bursts that predicts the advent of a flushing pheasant. A flushing pheasant might be the most startling thing in the world. Think of a fire truck painted like an iridescent rainbow, which did not approach from a distance but instead suddenly materialized under your feet and brushed against your pants on its way to an accident in the sky.

If you don't know what a flushing pheasant is like, there is nothing that can prepare you for it. Not that having seen it before can do much to brace you for seeing it again. If anything, the person who knows what to expect has even greater reason to feel anxious. If you do know what it's like, the prospect of a flush creeps into the day's every moment. When your foot breaks a stick beneath you, adrenaline surges at the thought – perhaps unconscious – that this could be it.

* * *

The flush of a pheasant is impossible to describe adequately to anyone who does not know what it is like. For those who do, any description is superfluous. All the same, I've tried to articulate it here, because I want to show that this singular event can provide a kind of conceptual anchor for other events, actions, and relationships in the life of the hunter. For some, a lot of life is lived with concepts that derive from the flush of a pheasant.

Begin with the moment after the pheasant flushes. Nothing signals the imminent arrival of the flush, so the hunt demands constant vigilance. Once the pheasant is in the air, only fractions of a second separate the successful shot from its securing a safe speed, altitude, and distance. The hunter must move with nearly automatic efficiency. There is no time for deliberation or margin for error. Every movement must be so ingrained that it can be executed unthinkingly. Just looking down the barrel of a shotgun involves a few layers of complexity. If you keep both eyes open, focusing on the bead at the end of the barrel will make the bird behind it appear distorted. If you focus on the bird, you can easily move your head off the barrel's "sight plain," disrupting the link between what-you-are-looking-at and where-the-gun-is-pointing. Once that connection is lost, you could shoot at a pheasant directly in front of you all afternoon and hit nothing but open sky. At the same time, you cannot simply close your less dominant eye without sacrificing depth perception, which you need to track a target moving in three-dimensional space. As you pick up the bird with your eyes, the barrel of your gun must be moving in time with the bird's flight. If you slow or stop your swing upon reaching the target, the bird will be somewhere else by the time the shot gets there. My father – who to my knowledge has never set brush to canvas – has always described the movement of the barrel as "painting."

Raising a shotgun is something like a work of art. It takes muscle memory to move one's body correctly when the pivotal moment finally arrives. The hunt infiltrates daily life. As with any discipline, it must be maintained regularly to ensure its reliability. When I was small, my parents would bring emptied guns into the living room. They would offer advice on raising them to a stationary target. They would raise both hands – as if from cradling an imagined shotgun – when ducks flew over the porch in the evening. After we adopted the practice of mounting an imaginary gun for an imaginary shot, my father would ask, "Did you have that one?" You should know whether a shot is a hit or a miss without having to pull the trigger.

Practice is only the beginning. In my family, Saturdays in the fall were all reserved for hunting. We came to know Arizona geography through a vocabulary of family names for hunting spots. At the height of their hunting powers, my parents had twenty-something named locations – so many that it was impossible to even hunt all of them in the weekends intervening between the opener in mid-October and season's close around the first of February. My parents named spots after groups of quail in the area, notable geographic features, or after their children or sometimes the occasional hunting guest. Years after we have left home, my parents continue to email reports of the conditions at "Ryan's Slough" and "Dillon's Pond" – locations knowable by those names only to the members of the family.

The hunt ties relationships together. In many cases, one simply cannot hunt alone. We learned to work the various duck calls so one person could have a gun at the ready while another was trying to tempt passersby into range. In the fall and winter, my parents regularly check a series of small cattle ponds scattered from the upper Sonoran Desert to Arizona's Mogollon Rim. "Glassing" the water from distance with binoculars, they look for small disturbances indicating ducks or geese. Should they find any, one of them carefully hides behind the pond's berm, while the other approaches from the upstream side in plain view. The strategy is for one person to flush the ducks over the other, within range of a shotgun. Birds are often too wary for anyone to approach directly to within shooting range, requiring the collaborative effort.

In hunting, such collaboration is pervasive. Rousseau uses a hunting metaphor to illustrate the possibility of – and challenges for – a rudimentary form of cooperation between persons. In his "stag hunt" game, each person must hold their position to capture a stag, which each hunter desires. Holding one's position means keeping faith with the other hunters, even if you see a hare run by that presents an easier individual-level opportunity. Rousseau's point is that it's challenging to maintain cooperation even when cooperation is in everyone's interests. Only one person would have to defect from the cooperative plan for the stag to escape, rendering everyone's work pointless. The temptation is magnified by the realization that everyone else is in the same predicament, and everyone knows that everyone is in the same predicament. If I know you know that I might defect, can I really trust you not to defect preemptively – especially once I consider that I just contemplated defecting, myself?

Though most hunting does not stare so far down the game tree, it does demand a lot of close coordination and mutual trust. The practice of "pushing and blocking" pheasants is similar to the hunting scenario Rousseau imagined. One group of hunters moves through a cornfield pressing the quarry toward another group of hunters. Everyone must walk carefully at the same rate and – most relevantly – avoiding shooting anyone on the opposing line. Most other forms of hunting have a collaborative component. Participants must maintain the correct location in the field – with its variable terrain and frequently high ground cover. Most of my family's outdoor activities were carried out with members of each separated group connected by an ill-functioning walkie-talkie, complete with our own makeshift code for signaling locations and plans.

With the need for multiple people, the hunt quickly becomes a space for family gathering. Wanting to show a good time to those who hunt less frequently, hunting becomes a central locus of planning for the entire year. Throughout my childhood and continuing to the present, my parents spend inordinate amounts of time "scouting" for new hunting spots to take members of the family who might only have a day or two to hunt. My father has called so many field rangers for the National Park Service and various Fish and Game agencies in states from North Dakota to Arizona that he – at one point – had an extensive network of government personnel with whom he was on a first name basis.

Each day of hunting conceals weeks – sometimes months – of planning. Each fall's pheasant hunt begins with a document – the "pheasant dossier" – plotting the GPS coordinates of likely locations. The construction of next year's dossier starts days after the close of this year's season. As fall approaches, preparation intensifies. My father once spent twenty-three days in a month getting up at 3:00 am to look for turkeys. My sister, mother, and brother had all drawn tags to hunt turkeys that year, leaving little choice in the matter. The end of that month featured the only time in my life I have ever seen Dad admit to exhaustion in the field. He gave up, but only for a single afternoon. But no one questions the worth of these efforts. After weddings, graduations, and the births of grandchildren, the happiest I've ever seen my parents was in the moments following my mother's successful hunt of a trophy Gould's Turkey. (The Gould's subspecies, native to a narrow swath of the borderlands between Arizona and Mexico, is America's largest turkey, and one of the Southwest's most elusive game tags.)

Because so much planning and preparation are invested in the hunt, its days are precious. The hunt displaced every holiday. My family celebrated Thanksgiving by pheasant hunting in Idaho, and Christmas by quail hunting on the Mexican border. For birthdays, one could pick the day's hunting spot, as well as the dinner grilled in the field before heading home. Neighbors would joke that my mother's end-of-year newsletter amounted to a series of photographs of each member of the family holding a dead animal (albeit respectfully). Such emphasis was not just for outsiders. Reminiscences about the past likewise centered on the hunt. Calls, text messages, and emails within the family are all about what hunting was like, and predictions about what it will be like. I'm tempted to say that every single phone call between members of my family features hunting. If false, it's only slightly an exaggeration. Steve, a man I knew in a nowhere, Wyoming trailer park – unemployed and on disability – used to talk about hunting every time I visited his home. He would say, "There's three seasons: huntin' season, plannin' season, and rememberin' season."

I will cut off from further detail, but – believe it or not – this is only the beginning. The hunter's concepts are built around the hunt. Geography, topography, and time are all oriented around when, where, and how to find game. "Good" weather is weather that conduces to good bird populations: cool and wet in the spring, but not so wet as to risk killing young chicks from exposure. Concepts of flora and fauna are likewise constructed: good trees and grass are those that yield the right combination of food and cover. As a child I learned to discern the tubers of wood sorrel as a prime food source for Mearn's Quail whenever I was pulling thorns out of my blue jeans. Relationships, commitments, and cooperation are organized around the hunt. Actions gain their meaning from their connection to hunting. The autobiographical story of one's life is straightforwardly a hunting story. Concepts – spatial, normative, temporal, metaphysical – are built around it. On one occasion in graduate school, I let my parents know that while I was planning to fly home for the holidays – due to an impending talk – I would not have time to go on the annual hunt. My father affirmed this supportively. "Do what you got to do," he said, before adding, "but then, why come at all?"

4. CONCEPTUAL DEVASTATION, REVISITED

Gun owners are notoriously uncompromising about their liberty to own and use guns. Much literature – in popular media and academic articles – tends to portray gun owners as some combination of unreasonable, inconsiderate, or paranoid. The idea is that gun owners are unwilling to understand that gun control advocates don't want to take their guns away – they just want some "reasonable," "common sense" limits on guns.

In the preceding section, I've tried to offer some materials from which we might better understand the psychology of the gun rights proponent. Psychologists find that all groups of people tend to be uncompromising about their symbolic values. We don't like making concessions with symbolic values because these values provide us with the tools to represent ourselves to ourselves. Our identities, as I described in the last chapter, provide us with the tools for acting automatically, which is enormously important. If we had to think through all of our actions individually, it would be difficult to stand back and see our life as a whole in a way that makes sense. We do that, instead, through the conceptual shorthand of identities. Someone with the identity of a "friend" does not need to think through how to interact over dinner, or at a social event. They can use their identity as friend to implicitly guide them in choosing what to say, how to act, when to laugh and when to remain silent, etc. (This is why it can sometimes be stressful to associate with others when our respective roles are unclear. If you don't know whether you are friends, colleagues, or prospective romantic partners, the smallest details of a social interaction might suddenly morph into locations of sharp anxiety.)

One might still wonder why all of this makes us uncompromising about our identities. A big problem is that we can be insecure about our identities. I might think that I'm a philosopher, but my identity as a philosopher might be vulnerable – a purely hypothetical example, to be sure! I might believe I'm a philosopher, but if others question whether my work is really philosophical, insinuate that I lack shared knowledge that philosophers are expected to possess, or refuse to refer to me as a philosopher, I might start to feel like my status a philosopher was open to question. Our identities are not things we can physically observe, like height or hair color. That's why we needed symbols to represent our identities in the first place. For similar reasons, we also need other people. Our thinking about our identities often reflects what we think others think about us.[6]

Our identities are not symbolic, but the ways we gain confidence in them are.[7] So if another person threatens the symbol we associate with our identity, it's easy to interpret that as a threat to the identity, itself. For the hunter, guns represent a – probably, the – central category of identity. As two scholars put it, the gun "brims with symbolic power far beyond its physical utility."[8] Accordingly, no one should be surprised when gun owners perceive what others regard as relatively minor incursions into their rights as deeply concerning. The difference is that outsiders don't see any symbolic content to various legislative constraints on gun ownership. Insiders see such constraints as significant, because they perceive them as a threat to their identity.

This matters for a couple of different reasons. First, it can help make sense of why gun owners respond negatively to policy changes that seem to make little material difference to their well-being. If someone threatens your identity and you treat their threat with equanimity, the message you send to yourself (among others, though less urgently) is that you don't regard the threat as serious. But if you don't regard the threat as serious that means you also don't regard the underlying identity as serious. However, if the identity in question is one of your core identities – in virtue of which other concepts, actions, and relationships can be understood – then this signals you don't take yourself seriously as a person. And that is a morally serious thing to be complicit in for anyone.[9]

Second, these concerns are amplified in a context where the potential impacts of a loss of a particular liberty are especially serious. My aim in this chapter has been to unpack just how serious the stakes are for gun owners. Gun owners make sense of a large swath of their lives through guns and their related activities. The issue is not the loss of a hobby. The issue is the loss of one's whole way of life. The gun owner stares down the prospect of conceptual devastation whenever that identity is threatened. And as I suggested earlier, conceptual devastation carries with it the prospect of making action difficult or impossible in a much more global way. Gun owners do cling to their guns and their religion.

Being puzzled about the overreaction of gun owners to 'commonsense' gun laws supposes that such laws don't actually threaten the actual practices that gun owners care about. So it matters a great deal whether the proposals of gun control proponents actually do threaten those practices. Several academic defenders of gun control note, for example, that even serious gun control is compatible with individuals being able to access and shoot firearms at "shooting clubs."[10]

How reassuring should this be? The answer is: Not very. For one thing, it's a suggestion that misunderstands both culture and geography in the West. Imagine telling a rancher outside of Big Piney that they could – in principle – drive two hours to shoot at an overpriced gun club in Jackson Hole. That doesn't even sound like a suggestion. It just sounds like an insult. It is not aware of the way in which guns figure into a life. Set aside though issues of practicality. What I hope should now be clear is why this kind of proposal is frightening. The advocate of gun control does not understand the social world of the gun owner. Perhaps more worrisome, this kind of gun control proposal betrays a second order ignorance: the gun control advocate does not appreciate the extent of their first-order misunderstanding of the gun owner's life. Just as we would have reason to worry about letting education policy be determined by someone who never went to school, or energy policy being decided by someone who can't remember that the Department of Energy even exists, it's reasonable for gun owners to worry about gun policy being influenced by gun control advocates who lack an understanding of the values at stake.

5. SOCIAL STANDING AND THE SUBLIME

Most political polarization in America today is geographic. Conservatives inhabit the rural interior of the country, and liberals dominate in most major cities. In this section I want to suggest that what liberal and socialist philosophers have to say about employment is exactly right about jobs in rural, predominantly conservative parts of the contemporary United States.

Their insight offers another way in to understanding the cultural value of guns. Strange as it may sound, I believe guns help gun owners have the kind of experiences that can help separate them from the distinctive bads associated with inequality.

On average, in rural parts of the country about one in five people have a college degree. That means that most workers will be doing jobs that – to put it frankly – are just a lot of work. Some of these jobs will, of course, contribute to the meaning of those who work them. But many will not. Many jobs involve labor that is largely unrewarding on its own terms. Here's the opening of political philosopher Sam Arnold's discussion of contemporary work:

> 'Most of us have jobs that are too small for our spirits.' Or so Studs Terkel concludes in Working, his classic collection of interviews with ordinary working people. Anyone familiar with contemporary occupational realities will find it hard to disagree with Terkel's remark. Millions toil in menial, unfulfilling jobs in factories, office parks, big box stores, restaurants and more. The work performed by these greeters, burger-flippers, assemblers and clerks is unskilled and repetitive; their workplaces, hierarchical and authoritarian. Vehicles for self-realization these jobs are not.[11]

Egalitarian philosophers think that this is a problem, and that the answer involves restructuring the workplace. I don't mean to weigh in for now about that solution, except to point out something relatively uncontroversial: whatever its merits, such change is not likely to arrive anytime soon.

The question is what to do in the meanwhile? For many people, there must be sources of meaning in life outside of one's work. But it's more than just that. Work creates a hierarchy of status, with some people on top and many others on the bottom. It's no surprise that being on the bottom can be bad for your sense of self-respect. As egalitarian-minded philosophers have long pointed out, seeing others in positions of disparate power and prestige to oneself is associated with a litany morally charged ills: domination, servility, etc.[12] Psychologists have likewise found that occupying low status positions has negative effects on emotions and on a person's ability to express them.[13]

Let's take for granted that (1) many jobs are not intrinsically meaningful, (2) such jobs often exist in spaces with a demoralizing level of hierarchy, and (3) these two features of the American workplace are not likely to go away anytime soon. Work takes up a great deal of our lives.[14] Given the amount of our time we dedicate to work, what is the best way of responding to this combination of features? One option is to try to get ahead. Call this the *striver's strategy*.[15] After all, the emotional harms associated with being at the bottom of the status hierarchy are not associated with being at the top of it.[16] This approach does not – cannot – work for everyone. The very nature of hierarchy is that space is limited at the top. The goods associated at the top are inherently positional – their value depends on *where one is in relation to other people*. While we can all try to follow the striver's strategy, we can't all follow it successfully. We cannot do it together.

Another possibility is that persons could find some way of conceiving of their life that didn't involve the hierarchy of the workplace. Call this the *escapist's strategy*. Escaping the workplace hierarchy is not as simple as deciding not to care. We often unintentionally think about ourselves in the same way we imagine people around us think about us. Often those people include co-workers or employers.

But what's the alternative? What one needs is a way in which to imagine oneself as inhabiting a completely different system of value. Religions can provide one such system of value.[17] But religions can also re-create their own hierarchies of status and power. Are there any ways of escaping hierarchy wholesale?

I want to briefly consider a kind of awe at the natural world, or what philosophers have referred to as "the sublime." The experience of the sublime classically involves two aspects: a sense of wonder at the vastness or grandeur of the natural world, and also a kind of uneasiness when comparing oneself against it. Kant explains the sublime this way:

> Bold, overhanging, and, as it were, threatening rocks, thunderclouds piled up the vault of heaven, borne along with flashes and peals, volcanos in all their violence and destruction, hurricanes leaving desolation in their track, the boundless ocean rising with rebellious force, the high waterfall of some mighty river, and the like, make our power of resistance of trifling moment in comparison with their might. But, provided our own position is secure, their aspect is all the more attractive for its fearfulness; and we readily call these objects sublime, because they raise the forces of the soul above the height of vulgar commonplace, and discover within us a power of resistance of quite another kind, which gives us courage to be able to measure ourselves against the seeming omnipotence of nature.[18]

Sandra Shapshay explains Kant's point as underscoring on the one hand our insignificance in contrast to what she calls "the grand scheme of nature."[19] On the other hand this very recognition "reveals that we can transcend nature as moral agents and systematic knowers."[20] For Kant, experiences of the sublime are ambivalent. We notice how small we are in comparison to nature. At the same time – or just a moment later – our awareness of that very recognition reveals that we have a remarkable capacity to entertain thoughts of extraordinary phenomena. And seeing ourselves as being able to have thoughts like that reveals something extraordinary in ourselves. Our capacity to conceptualize things far beyond us is something we might not have otherwise noticed. So the experience of the sublime diminishes our sense of ourselves, but then elevates us as well.

Whatever one makes of Kant's particular explanation, the phenomenology of this experience seems very relatable. When we look out over a vast canyon or find ourselves in complete solitude under the night sky, our response involves both wonder and something like disorientation or fear. One might call it a kind of emotional vertigo.[21]

Many people recognize this experience. My conjecture is that experiencing the sublime could help to counteract the stigmatizing effects of workplace hierarchy. Recall that the problem is about how relationships are structured. That was bad because it affected how people see themselves: as subservient and irrelevant components in a system they don't control. If the problem is about how people are brought to see themselves in relation to their work life, then perhaps (a part of) a solution is to find a different kind of identity to focus on. And my conjecture is that this is what the sublime furnishes. If people can think of themselves in relation to Kant's starry heavens above, or just in relation to the natural world of forest ecosystems or songbird migrations, then they might have less default pressure to see themselves as the hapless underling of a boss at work. There's actually some psychology to support this idea. Appreciating nature can contribute to the meaning of your life in a distinctive way.[22] Experiences of awe at the natural environment predict a reduction in social dominance orientation.[23] Put simply, if you can find value in nature, it can take the pressure off to climb the rungs of a corporate ladder at work.

What does all this have to do with guns? Of course, most people will likely be able to experience the sublime without literally finding things in nature to shoot. But I want to take seriously the common refrain among hunters that they find sublime experiences in the hunt. To hunt is to see oneself as not just an observer, but as a participant in the natural world. Now, what I am saying may run close to hubris, which I want to avoid. I'm not saying that the hunter should imagine themselves as a kind of wild animal. Humans – for better or worse – are all caught up in global supply chains of foods and services. But in a suitably modest sense, the hunter can see themselves in another way as well. They can reckon the kind of creature they are alongside the coyote or Cooper's Hawk, rather than only alongside the other people with whom they work. They can access an identity that is at once less adversarial and potentially more meaningful than their work identity. There is no one else against whom they are competing for raises, positions, or status. It gives them an identity that doesn't depend on how others see them at all. Further, it offers a way of seeing oneself that is elevating rather than stigmatizing or diminishing.

When my dad came back from being thrown out of the Coca Cola plant, he was remarkably sanguine about it. Telling the story about the quail he heard from the parking lot made him realize that there was something remarkable about him that his successes or failures as a salesman couldn't touch. In a rare moment approximating self-praise, he reflected, "I don't think most people would've heard the quail."

6. CONCLUSION

Here is the argument of this chapter. We need to act, and we also need to shape our actions together into narratives that make sense to us. To do this we need a set of concepts to interpret and make sense of our actions, in connection to our own past and future lives, and in connection with the people with whom we live those lives. Second, we need a kind of assurance about our place in the world. We need to know that we matter to the people around us, and – most of all – to ourselves. We need to be secure in our own standing in a social world that we care about. These two ideas – the capacity to act and security of having a place in the world – go into giving a life meaning. For some people, these two essential constituents of meaning are closely tied to a way of life that centers on guns. Guns can help people to act, and to have status in a world of their own creating. So guns can help people to create meaning in their lives.

Of course, it will here be obvious that I have said nothing about how large the set of people is for whom this is true. Let us grant for the argument that such people are rare. I don't see how that makes the case any less important. Rare ways of life are exactly what we need rights to protect.

Guns as a Deontological Right

3

Is there a personal right to own a gun? In this chapter I will argue that there is. Most people acquire guns out of a concern for personal security, and most philosophical debate about guns centers on whether there is a right to a gun for self-defense. So it makes sense to start with the question of whether the right to self-defense supports a right to own a gun. The fault lines in this debate are now well established. Pro-gun philosophers argue that depriving people of guns deprives them of the means necessary for self-defense, and so violates their right to physical security. Anti-gun philosophers argue that given what we know about the empirical consequences of guns in society, the government better protects rights, on balance, through restrictions on private gun ownership. I'll call this the *central debate* over guns.

My first aim in this chapter will be to show that the central debate highlights a big picture theoretical tension. If you believe the government should maximize the satisfaction of rights over all – that is, that if governments should be consequentialists about rights – then it will be hard to motivate the pro-gun case. On the other hand, if you think that rights should be respected even if honoring them does not result in the greatest realization of rights overall, then the demand to respect an individual's right to self-defense will be hard to resist. In other words, a lot will depend on whether one is a consequentialist about rights, or a deontologist about rights.

DOI: 10.4324/9781003434818-4

It may seem odd that such a high-level theoretical divide will be required to resolve practical questions about rights to guns. And in fact, proponents of gun control have long maintained that if one grants the gun rights advocates' premises about rights in general, the case for restrictions can still succeed anyway. I disagree. If there is a deontological right to self-defense, then there is a right to own a gun.

1. SELF-DEFENSE

The most common reason for owning a gun is self-defense. The idea that individual persons have a right to defend themselves is commonplace in contemporary American society, and it has a long, philosophical history as well. John Locke famously argued that all individuals have a natural right to their physical body.[1] Locke reasoned that if rights could not be defended with force, it wouldn't mean much to say one had a "right" to something. Locke thought that a system of rights that didn't allow for defense wouldn't make sense, so he concluded that individuals must be able to defend their rights – at least enough to make violating a right an "ill bargain" for the offender. Locke was interested in the right to punish others, an entitlement he referred to as the "executive power."

Whatever one thinks about the Lockean view, a more limited right to self-defense remains widely accepted. Michael Huemer, the most influential contemporary philosophical defender of a personal right to own a gun, takes the right to self-defense as starting point.[2] Huemer argues that if individuals have a right to defend themselves, this right must extend as well to the means of self-defense. To make this point, he imagines a potential victim who keeps a gun by their bed. Imagine that a killer sneaks into the room to assassinate the victim. Sensing the danger, the victim reaches for the gun. However, just at that moment an accomplice snatches the gun away.[3]

The accomplice is guilty of a serious rights violation. Even though the accomplice does nothing to the victim besides deprive them of the needed means of self-defense, we intuitively judge the accomplice much the same as we do the killer. The accomplice may not kill the victim, but he is still guilty of something approaching murder in moral seriousness. Huemer's point is that a government imposing a ban on guns is analogous to being in the role of the accomplice. If the government deprives people of the means of self-defense, it is violating their rights in a morally serious way.

Let's call this the basic argument from self-defense:

(1) Each person has a right to self-defense.
(2) Depriving someone of access to an effective means to self-defense violates their right to self-defense.
(3) Guns are an effective means of self-defense.
(4) Legal restrictions against private gun ownership deprive people of access to guns.
(5) So, legal restrictions against private gun ownership violate the right to self-defense.

Premise (1) is taken for granted. (2) is supported by cases like those just described. (3) may be empirically controversial, and I will get into it in more detail in Chapter 5. For now, the idea is just that if someone is trying to physically harm you, a gun offers one means of protecting yourself. (4) targets legislation that criminalizes gun ownership.

2. AN OBJECTION

The skeptic might deny premise (4) in the basic argument. Huemer anticipates that skeptics will not see a legislative ban on guns as analogous to the accomplice in the murder case. However, it isn't immediately clear why the differences between them should be morally relevant. The government imposing a ban deprives people of guns well in advance of when they are needed for defense, rather than mere moments before. But this difference in timing seems irrelevant. (One can imagine the accomplice sneaking into the room to steal the gun a month before the murder, but this does nothing to attenuate his complicity.) Likewise, the government does not know the identities of those who will lose their ability to defend themselves, but this also doesn't seem to matter. You can violate someone's rights without knowing your victim's particular identity.

A more serious objection is that the government's policy is aimed at saving lives from gun violence, while the accomplice's is not. This might be understood as one way of denying (2) in the basic argument. And for all we know – at least given the way I've sketched the self-defense argument here – the government's policy may actually succeed. It may save lives on balance, and it may reduce the total number of rights violations. Several philosophers have thought that this objection furnishes a powerful rebuttal against Huemer's argument. Jeff McMahan writes:

> Imposing a ban on guns, [opponents] argue, would be tantamount to taking a person's gun from her just as someone is about to kill her. But this is a defective analogy. Although a prohibition would deprive people of one effective means of self-defense, it would also ensure there would be far fewer occasions on which a gun would be useful or even necessary for self-defense . . . Guns are only one means of self-defense, and self-defense is only one means of achieving security against attack. It is the right of security against attack that is fundamental.

A policy that unavoidably deprives a person of one means of self-defense but on balance substantially reduces her vulnerability to attack is therefore respectful of the more fundamental right from which the right of self-defense is derived.[4]

There are a couple of different ways in which we might interpret this objection. One possibility is to hear the objection as holding that a gun ban is justified if it maximizes the protection of rights overall. On this interpretation, it might be that there are a few occasions on which someone is deprived of the means they need to defend themselves, and so their right to self-defense is violated. However, this is just the price that must be paid for a safer society. As McMahan says, "there would be far fewer occasions" in which guns would be needed for self-defense, because the ban on guns would reduce the total amount of harm produced by guns, and also – by hypothesis – the total number of rights violations.

I'll describe this view as a kind of consequentialism about rights. (I'm not attributing it to McMahan, but just using it for illustrative purposes.) The consequentialist about rights holds that it is ok to violate the rights of some, so long as it minimizes the number of rights violations overall. The problem for this interpretation of the objection is that it saddles the defender of gun control with an extremely controversial commitment in moral theory. Most philosophers do not accept that promoting rights overall counts as a satisfactory justification for violating an individual's rights. Huemer invokes a common objection to utilitarianism to make this point. He imagines a town that would descend into violent riots unless someone is punished for a murder.[5] The sheriff, unable to find the actual perpetrator, can either punish an innocent bystander or do nothing at all.

If the sheriff punishes the bystander, the riots will be quelled and the total number of rights violations, overall, will be minimized. If the sheriff does nothing, the innocent bystander will not be falsely accused, but the total number of unjust deaths will increase as violence ensues.

Punishing a bystander is unjustified. You cannot violate one person's rights, even if doing so will reduce the total number of rights violations. In so arguing, Huemer defends a standard view among normative theorists. Consequentialism about rights is false. This is because it is a conceptual feature of rights that they cannot be traded off directly against each other. Frances Kamm refers to this feature as "inviolability."[6] Persons not only have rights, but those rights are inviolable. That is, it is not permissible to violate their rights even for the greater satisfaction of rights overall. There need not be anything special about the particular bystander in Huemer's imagined town. All persons have inviolable rights. No one should violate another's rights for the sake of making the world better in consequentialist terms – even when that includes making the world better for rights generally.

So much for consequentialism about rights. However, another – more charitable – interpretation of McMahan's objection is available. On this interpretation, it is not only the case that people are made safer overall, but that each individual person is made safer. As McMahan says, the point of a right to self-defense is to protect one's physical security. So what really matters is this security; the way it is brought about is of secondary importance. If a gun control regime makes each person safer in expectation than they otherwise would be, then the state is actually not like the accomplice who steals away the gun. While the accomplice renders the victim vulnerable to attack, the state makes people less vulnerable. The idea is that if the government reduces the number of firearms overall while also providing sufficient law enforcement protection, even those who would have used guns to defend themselves will be safer with gun control.

Under this interpretation, there are no tradeoffs between separate individuals, so there is no complaint based on each person's inviolability. However, the problem for this interpretation of the argument is that it requires an extremely demanding empirical claim. How plausible is it that each person would be made safer by a strict gun control regime? Huemer regards it as "certainly false" that each individual could be made safer.[7] All that is required to make this claim false is that there is some citizen who would be safer by owning a gun than they would be under the gun control regime. There are several reasons. First, as Huemer points out, it is very easy to think of likely counterexamples. Imagine a person with an abusive ex-spouse who has threatened violence, and who lacks the physical means to defend themselves without a gun (suppose they are physically much smaller than their ex). Such a person might well want a gun for self-protection, and it seems plausible that they could be safer with a gun than if forced to wait for the police. In general, the number of defensive gun uses is such as to make it extremely likely – at the least – that there are such cases. (One in four gun owners report using a gun for defensive purposes at some point in their life.)[8] Third, even if it is in principle possible that everyone would be made safer by the gun control regime, that is a long way from showing that everyone in contemporary American society would be made safer under a gun ban. (I will discuss this in more detail in Chapter 8.)

The moral of this story – at least so far – is that the case for a gun ban depends on some controversial commitments. If rights consequentialism is true, and if a gun ban would in fact be the best system for protecting rights overall, then sweeping gun control might be justified. But rights consequentialism is a philosophically ambitious outlook, and it faces widespread opposition. It's possible to make the case against gun rights without it, but then the proponent of gun control must turn to controversial empirical claims. In short, the case for gun control will often deny commonly accepted claims about the nature of rights and the inviolability of persons.

3. REVAMPING THE OBJECTION

Even some philosophers who favor expansive gun control have agreed that it is unlikely to make everyone safer. In a sophisticated recent contribution to the debate, Dustin Crummett and Philip Swenson grant that while "gun control may make people safer on average, it does not make each person safer," so they agree that Huemer's self-defense based argument can withstand the criticism discussed in the last section.[9] However, Crummett and Swenson believe that the objection fails only because we haven't yet thought about the analogy between the government and the accomplice in the right way. Like McMahan, they think that analogy is misleading. Their explanation for why it is misleading gets into the weeds of a more complicated philosophical puzzle, but the detour is worth taking. Seeing how their revised objection works will help us get to the heart of the disagreement between the gun control advocate and proponents of gun rights.

Crummett and Swenson hold that the government is not like the accomplice because the government does not know the particular identities of those who are made safer by gun control and those who made less safe. Recall that in Huemer's original case, the accomplice steals the gun away from a specific person, thereby rendering that person vulnerable to attack. While a gun prohibition would take guns from people, the government would not know whom it was exposing to threats. As a result, Crummett and Sewenson suggest, the government is not trading off some rights for the sake of others when it acts to promote security overall. And for that reason, the government is not flouting the inviolability of each person.

Why think that simply not knowing who was affected in what way could make such a difference? To get to the bottom of this matter, we'll have to introduce another famous philosophical case: the trolley problem. (Philosophers love hypothetical cases, but it makes good psychological sense to use them. Researchers have found that when we discuss simple cases, we can do so with less ideological baggage than when we talk about controversial political issues directly. That means there's a better chance for finding common ground.) In the classic trolley problem, you find yourself on a footbridge as a trolley approaches. The trolley is about to collide into five people tied to the tracks below, but if you push a large person next to you off the bridge, you can save their lives. Unfortunately, you will kill the person, but there is no other way to save the innocent lives of the five tied to the tracks.[10]

In the classic trolley problem case, we confront a tradeoff like the one we've been considering so far. Should you violate one person's right to life to save the lives of a larger number of others? The complexity Crummett and Swenson introduce is to imagine a version of this case in which we don't know whose rights we would be violating and whose we would be protecting. Following the philosopher Caspar Hare, Crummett and Swenson consider a version of the trolley problem in which there are again six people at risk – call them A, B, C, D, E, and F.[11] One of them is beside you on the bridge, and the other five are stranded on the track. However, each person has been stuffed – unharmed – into a suitcase. (I realize this hypothetical is getting more outlandish, but bear with me – it actually will get at an important point.) The question you now face is whether you should push the person in the suitcase in front of the trolley to save the other five.

Why think it makes any difference at all that you don't know the identities of the individuals? Hare introduces this variant of the trolley problem to show that now, if you are only concerned about the well-being of one person, then it makes sense to push the suitcase. So for example, if I only want to maximize the chance of saving A, and I push the suitcase, then I have a 5/6 chance of saving A and a 1/6 chance of killing A. Notice also that your situation is exactly the same with respect to B, C, D, and all the rest. So for each person, the thing that gives that person the best chance of being saved is to push the suitcase. And if pushing the suitcase makes sense from the point of view of considering each person's interests separately, then there is no conflict in interests from your point of view. That means you aren't treating anyone's rights as violable for the sake of the overall good.

Crummett and Swenson argue that the government's situation is similar to your situation in the suitcases version of the trolley problem.[12] If Hare is right, then you should push the suitcase in front of the trolley, because that is what you ought to do with respect to your relationship with any given person. And if something is what you ought to do from the point of view of any person's good, then that must be the morally right thing to do. Likewise, the government of a huge country like the United States may not know the particular identities of those lives saved and lost from any given policy, but if it acts so as to maximize the total number of lives saved, then it is acting as it should from the point of view of any particular citizen.

This is an impressive innovation in the guns debate. It threatens to show that the argument from an individual right to self-defense goes wrong from the start. The question is whether adding the anonymity in the suitcases version really succeeds at showing there is no conflict in rights. After all, although you do not know the identity of the person in the suitcase you will push in front of the trolley, suppose we assume that the person in the suitcase does know. This would have the advantage of making the case arguably more analogous to the government and gun owners. Although the government does not know whose self-defense is compromised by restrictions, it is much more likely that those deprived of the means of self-defense *do* know who they are.

Once we make clear that the person in the suitcase on the bridge knows they're in a position to be sacrificed, it's obvious that pushing the suitcase is not in their interest. And if we know that they know they will be sacrificed, there is no reason to presume they would consent to our pushing. From our point of view, we increase A's odds of surviving by pushing. But if A is in the suitcase we push, then we kill someone without their consent. It's hard to feel ok about that. As Kieren Setiya writes in a rejoinder to Hare:

> Being killed without consent may not do more harm to A than being allowed to die. But the moral objection to killing is more profound. It is not about A's interests but her rights . . . [Y]ou must weight A's prospects for survival against her right to be free of unwanted fatal intervention. Pushing . . . improves her odds of living, on your evidence, but risks killing her against her will.[13]

Simply not knowing whose rights we are giving up for the greater protection of rights overall doesn't mean we aren't making a tradeoff. Crummett and Swenson suggest that perhaps even if those whose guns are taken by the government do not consent in real life, they would hypothetically consent to a policy that makes people safer in expectation.[14] But again, just like the person who knows she's in the unlucky suitcase, citizens who keep guns for self-defense may well know that the policy makes them less safe. It matters little that the government doesn't know who they are.

Suppose we grant that gun control will increase the protection of rights overall. I believe we cannot avoid thinking that this policy still deprives some people of the means needed for self-defense. We cannot assume they consent to this deprivation. That means the policy violates their rights. There is just no getting around the thought that a gun control regime engages in some kind of rights consequentialism. And if you believe – as I do – that persons are inviolable, this is a serious problem. That we are promoting the rights of others does not permit us to violate the rights of some.

4. CONCLUSION

Even though many philosophers are skeptical of the right to own a gun for self-defense, my conclusion so far is that the case for this right can only be defeated by undertaking controversial philosophical assumptions. If you believe that we should promote rights overall, and you believe gun control does that, then I have no quarrel with you. But many people believe that rights are inviolable, and think they can still support restrictive gun control. That view, I think, is a mistake. If there is an inviolable right to self-defense, then there is a right to own a gun.

Guns as a Liberal Right

4

The last chapter argued for a deontological right to own a gun. This chapter will turn to another way of grounding gun rights. I will next argue that if we accept a broadly Rawlsian view about individual liberties, then the case for a liberty right to own a gun is comparably strong to many so-called "basic liberties" the Rawlsian defends. Among philosophers, few Rawlsians will put gun rights on the list of basic liberties. However, I don't think there is a principled case for excluding gun rights. The case for a liberty right to a gun is just as good as for other liberty rights of traditional liberal concern.

In the second part of the chapter, I will grant (for the sake of the argument) that there is no right to own a gun at all. Does it follow that gun control is morally permissible? I will argue that it does not. Liberal philosophers routinely argue that criminalization is wrong, even when they doubt there is an individual right to what is criminalized. I believe that according to standard liberal views, even if there is no right to own a gun, legal restrictions on guns will be largely unjust in the actual world.

1. GUN RIGHTS AS A BASIC LIBERTY

Many people want to own guns because they value activities that guns make possible (a point I argued at some length in the foregoing chapters). Or perhaps people mistakenly

71 **Guns as a Liberal Right**

DOI: 10.4324/9781003434818-5

believe a gun will provide important protection, when in fact – let's suppose – that isn't true. Gun control advocates often argue as if showing that gun rights did not really promote personal security would somehow undermine these rights. I see no reason to think this is so. Recall the comparison with religion. Suppose we could confidently show that some religion did not – contrary to the beliefs of its practitioners – yield any greater chance of salvation after this life. This might be disappointing, but certainly it would not show that the religious practice didn't deserve protection, or that the liberty to participate in this religion was not morally important. Respecting people would still require leaving them alone to practice their religion as they chose, even if it didn't "work" in the way they hoped.

I think something similar can be said about gun rights. Even if guns do not – in fact – provide a valuable means to self-defense, the liberty to have a gun can still matter a great deal. It can still deserve protection, and violating it can still be morally serious. I believe the right to own a gun has as good a basis in liberal theory as any other liberty-right that liberal philosophers care about.

To argue for this conclusion, the first step is to set out how philosophers argue for liberty-rights. Rawls introduced the concept of "basic liberties," which he used to pick out those liberties that were in some way morally important or privileged. The idea is that some liberties matter more than others, and the basic liberties are those that deserve special protection by justice. Rawls argued that these liberties could not be traded off to promote other values, like welfare, economic growth, or fairness. They also could not be sacrificed for the sake of non-basic liberties. If tradeoffs must be made, it is only just to sacrifice a basic liberty to protect another basic liberty. For Rawls, the basic liberties could be given as a list, which included liberty of thought and conscience, freedom of association, a right to personal property, the rights to vote and hold elected office, and rights to due process and equal protection under the law.[1]

The list of basic liberties, along with the refusal of tradeoffs, can help one understand a lot of broadly liberal political principles. For instance, imagine if shuttering an unpopular church would improve business for a small tourist community. Even if it would advantage more people than it would disadvantage, it would still be wrong for town officials to close down the local congregation. Or imagine if censoring an unpopular political opinion would make most people much happier. Again, gains in welfare don't justify restricting free expression or conscience. We should not trade off basic liberties for other political values, however important they might be. As Rawls explained at the beginning of *A Theory of Justice*, justice has a value that the good of whole of society cannot override.[2]

Basic liberties enjoy a special priority. The question now is: Why should all and only the liberties on Rawls's list count as basic? Rawlsians answer this question by appealing the role that basic liberties play in an individual's life. Rawls held that basic liberties are essential for the development of what he called a person's two "moral powers." The moral powers, in turn, include a "sense of justice" (or what Rawls sometimes called "reasonableness") and the capacity to develop a conception of the good (or what Rawls called "rationality"). The sense of justice is moralized; it refers to a person's ability to live with others according to fair terms of cooperation. A conception of the good involves having a set of values that organize and guide one's life over time. Having a conception of the good is something like being the author of one's own life.[3]

On Rawls's view, if a liberty is necessary for (or perhaps: relevantly promotes or facilitates) the achievement of the two moral powers, then the liberty counts as a basic liberty. Jason Brennan calls this the "moral powers test," as it is meant to provide a principled explanation for why some liberties are on the list and why others don't make the cut.[4] It makes sense that some of the items on Rawls's list really are supported by the moral powers test. For example, freedom of conscience and association are likely important – for many people – to formulating and living a life of their own choosing.[5] In this way, they are significant means to developing one's own conception of the good.

What should a defender of the moral powers test say about a proposed right to own a gun? First consider this question with respect to developing a sense of justice. As I argued in the last chapter, I believe that gun ownership can – although certainly need not – play an important role in establishing and maintaining relationships of cooperation. Gun owners have especially warm feelings toward each other. Guns provide a way of signaling a person's full membership within some communities. So it is plausible, I think, that a right to own guns could help to bring about the conditions that bolster a sense of justice.

However, I don't need to rely on any connection between owning guns and developing a capacity to cooperate with others. There's a much stronger case for thinking that – for many supporters of gun rights, at least – there is a connection between the right to own a gun and developing a conception of the good. To start, it will help to specify in slightly greater detail what counts as a "conception of the good." Here I will point to three criteria, which I don't think should be especially controversial.

(a) Choosing and pursing one's own ends. If individuals are able to "form, revise, and pursue" a conception of the good, they must be able to select ends.[6] "Ends" in this sense are goals or objectives. Choosing and pursuing ends involves being able to decide which goals or objectives to adopt, and then take the means to achieve those ends.

(b) Self-Authorship. Some philosophers have argued that having a conception of the good entails being the author of one's own life, where such authorship includes being able to define one's own identity and determine one's own place in society.[7]

(c) Narrative Control. Having one's own conception of the good may also mean being able to decide how events in one's life fit together, or form a coherent story or narrative.[8]

People disagree over what's required for forming and pursing a conception of the good. For our purposes, disagreement shouldn't matter too much. However we understand the idea, access to guns will fit squarely within its scope. Admittedly, this will only be true "for some people," but this is equally true for the paradigm of basic liberties. Many people don't care about engaging in politics, and many people don't care about practicing a religion, yet both of these are counted officially on Rawls's list.[9]

How does a putative right to own a gun fit with these criteria? Here I hope that the elaboration given in the preceding two chapters will prove useful. First take the idea of choosing and pursuing one's own ends. As I described in Chapter 1, the liberty to own and use a gun is an essential means to a variety of final ends or objectives shared by diverse groups of citizens. Guns are necessary to these ends. If individuals were denied access to guns, the associated goals and activities would be frustrated.

Second, consider the idea of self-authorship. Self-authorship includes deciding both one's own identity and one's place in society.[10] As I sketched in Chapter 2, guns can be important to both projects. Guns help individuals to conceptually structure their lives, determining how they will think about a host of interconnected values. Identity, as psychologists use that concept, has to do with what you do automatically, rather than what you manually think about doing. Guns are deeply connected to those parts of an individual's agency that work without conscious attention. They are, in that way, built into the individual's identity. This isn't just about the basic actions and bodily movements required to shoot. It also has to do with the ways in which individuals value themselves and find their place in the world. Guns provide entry into a set of valuing practices. In this way, guns contribute to the second component of self-authorship: determining one's place or status in society. As I described in the last chapter, many gun enthusiasts lack other markers of status or meaning. Owning a gun confers a sense of place within a group and value in contributing to it. I outlined how this works with a few stories, but my vignettes fit within the frame utilized by sociological work.[11]

Third, guns are important to the narrative control of gun owners over their own lives. Guns figure significantly into how individuals organize their lives across time. They highlight some of the most prominent events in the lives of gun owners. They connect those events over time through a multitude of smaller activities. The lifestyle built around gun ownership features activities with a common narrative arc. Individual gun owners work at developing a suite of related skills in anticipation of the pivotal moment when those skills will all be needed at once. The best narratives are sometimes those that require sacrifice and effort in pursuit of a final achievement, and this is exactly how these activities work. In this way, guns can contribute to the narrative unity of the gun owner's life.

Much of the last two chapters aimed to support these points. It seems quite clear that for gun owners, guns will play a meaningful role in forming and pursuing a conception of the good. My guess is that the skeptic will doubt whether guns are strictly *necessary* for having the capacity to form and pursue a conception of the good. "Certainly," the skeptic might say, "as much as a person may care about firearms, they would still be able to develop the capacity for this moral power if they lacked access to guns." And this is true enough, but I don't think that it gives my opponent much ground. Why not? The same objection can be deployed against literally any basic liberty.[12] Certainly one can develop the capacity to form and pursue a conception of the good without any particular civil or political liberty. As Jason Brennan points out, individuals in the most politically repressive societies still exercise both of Rawls's moral powers, so it doesn't appear – as an empirical matter – that any liberty is a necessary condition for people to acquire them.[13]

Here is a dilemma for the liberal opponent of gun rights. Either the opponent can deny that gun rights count as basic liberties, but at the price of holding that there really aren't any basic liberties after all. Alternatively, if the opponent wants to keep the category of "basic liberty" intact, then the case that access to and use of guns will count as a basic liberty is – I think – about as strong as the case for any basic liberty. I have no quarrel with the liberal who doesn't really believe in basic liberties altogether, but accepts a more welfarist or consequentialist way of thinking about political liberty. But for the person who does believe in significant, nonconsequentialist liberty rights, I think it is hard to draw the boundaries of this category in a way that keeps guns out.

2. AN OBJECTION

I've defended a liberal right to own guns based on the meaning or significance of that right to the life of the gun owner. This argument drew on the claim from Chapter 1 that guns have a distinctive symbolic value. Here I want to pause to consider an objection: What about symbolic values that are also morally objectionable? It is important to be clear that I am not defending just *anything* that people attach symbolic significance to. Some things can give meaning to your life, but are also morally wrong. There is no special right to morally wrong actions, however important they may be to a person.

Here is a case to motivate the idea.[14] In 2010, an Alabama football fan named Harvey Updyke poisoned two oak trees on Toomer's Corner, at Auburn University.[15] Generations of Auburn fans had long celebrated victories under the trees. When Alabama lost their rivalry game that year to Auburn, Updyke recounted that he wanted to do something that would "make Auburn people hate me as much as I hate them." He called in to a radio program to boast about his actions. Despite efforts to save them, the trees died later that year. The soil surrounding them was excavated, but a replacement tree later died as well.

Without question, Alabama football had great value to Updyke. His conception of the good was built around it, let's even suppose. It seems likely that his loyalty to Alabama contributed to the meaning of his life. However, we don't want to say that he had a right to poison Auburn's cherished oak trees. In general, we do not have rights to violate the rights of others.

This is an important qualification on liberty rights. If a value is pursued in a morally impermissible way, then this cancels or silences the reasons supporting it. You might have reasons to celebrate a friend's birthday (given the special meaning of their birthday in their life), but you can't steal from someone else to buy a present. There are reasons to celebrate your team's victory or sorrow in their defeat – just not in ways that violate others' rights.

What this means is that the liberal right to own and use a gun does not extend to performing any actions the violate the rights of others. Facts about symbols and meaning can show why some liberties are important, but they of course do not provide a complete account of the rights people have. In the next section, I will focus on how the moral permissibility of gun ownership is related to the justification for a legal right to own a gun.

3. RIGHTS AGAINST CRIMINALIZATION

So far, I've argued for a right to own a gun. But what if there is no particular right to own a gun? It could still be wrong to impose criminal sanctions against gun ownership or use. It could even still be wrong to impose criminal sanctions against owning or using specific types of guns. This is because persons have general rights against being punished when they've done nothing wrong, and there is nothing in principle wrong with owning and responsibly using a gun. In this section, I will defend a version of this argument, as follows:

(1) Each person has a right not to be punished if they've done nothing morally wrong.
(2) It is not morally wrong to own a gun.
(3) So, it is wrong to punish someone for owning a gun.

Let's start with premise (1). We all have a right not to be punished. Here I'll start by following the influential work of Douglas Husak on the topic. Once the general argument is on the table, it will be easier to see how it applies to gun ownership.

Premise (1) affirms a right against punishment. This premise seems relatively uncontroversial. Punishments do two things. They impose a kind of hard treatment on the recipient, extending to imprisonment. Second, they express indignation or resentment.[16] Of course, we express these attitudes in our ordinary moral lives, and it's common to think that it's appropriate to do so whenever we've been wronged by a morally responsible agent.[17] Reactive attitudes communicate to an offender that we not only judge their action to be wrong, but that we also regard its wrongness as our business in some way. We are entitled to hold them to account. If the wrongdoer appreciates this, then their uptake of our resentment makes appropriate a corresponding feeling of guilt on their part. Punishment plays these functions as well, but in a much more serious way. By combining hard treatment – or the coercive imposition of penalties through physical force – with expressive indignation, it signals a stronger level of accountability on the part of the wrongdoer.

In the ordinary case, we think that it is morally inappropriate to even resent someone who has done nothing wrong. Intuitively, then, we also ought not punish persons who haven't done anything wrong. If it is wrong to punish people, then persons have a right against being punished. Husak makes the further point that the right against punishment is in an important sense much more important than many other rights.[18] If you had to choose which of your rights to have violated, it would be rational to choose almost any other right ahead of the right against wrongful punishment. Consider, for example, having your freedom of speech constrained, or being prevented from assembling with your chosen political or religious group, or having your property unlawfully taken. Most people would prefer almost any of these to being criminally punished. If your other rights are violated, you can continue to lead a life of your own choosing, albeit in a constrained way. However, being imprisoned or physically punished can prevent an agent from pursuing any of their ends at all. It offers a global threat to the authorship of their own life. Accordingly, the right against wrongful punishment should be seen as especially stringent. Maybe some rights can be overridden, but not this one – or at least, it would take a lot to justify wrongfully punishing someone. We regard it as wrong to punish the innocent, even if doing so would result in very substantial gains in well-being overall.

Perhaps, however, the right to punishment is not overridden, but the right against being punished is somehow cancelled by owning a gun. This takes us to premise (2): that owning and using a gun is not morally wrong. Although there's a strong right against punishment, this right is limited to prohibiting unjust punishment. Violating the rights of others can cancel or forfeit one's claim against hard treatment.[19] The question is whether owning or using a gun might cancel one's protection against punishment. On the face of it, possession and responsible use of firearms doesn't seem to raise any moral issues. For the most part, even proponents of strict gun control don't argue that merely owning or using a gun is morally objectionable. After all, one can imagine owning a gun in a way that withholds from any interference or risk of interference in the lives of others. The gun can be kept in a safe, taken securely to areas where it can be shot safely, and then returned – all without the notice of anyone else. Compare with ordinary daily actions like driving to work or teaching a lecture. No matter how careful I am on the road, there's some residual risk that I'll be involved in a car accident. And no matter how conscientious I am in class, there's a chance that some stray phrase will offend a student. In actions like these, it feels like I'm risking moral conflict to a greater degree than I am by mere ownership and use of a gun. And yet, we think that driving to work and teaching lectures are morally permissible actions. So I think there should be at least a presumption in favor of premise (2).

There are a couple of ways in which philosophers might try to resist the claim that gun ownership is morally acceptable. First, one might hold that gun ownership does do something wrong, but to a small degree – such that it might go unnoticed. Thomas Metcalf, for example, argues that guns are like industrial pollution.[20] Pollution is appropriately subject to regulation because polluting imposes a harm on others, even if any individual polluter's contribution only negligibly contributes to that harm. Likewise, one might think that gun ownership collectively imposes a harm, even if one's own contribution to that harm is negligible.

Metcalf puts pressure on a premise that gun rights advocates have usually taken for granted. His critique holds some philosophical plausibility, and in a moment I'll consider what happens if we grant it. However, I am so far not persuaded, because I think it is false that gun ownership negligibly contributes to harm. In the case of pollution, there is a mechanistic connection between merely engaging in the activity, and negligibly contributing to the harm. There is no way to run a combustion engine, for example, without also polluting. In the case of guns, there is no such connection. We can imagine everyone possessing and safely shooting guns without anyone incurring harm. Of course, this ideal is unfortunately out of reach. But its possibility reveals a relevant difference with the pollution case: owning a gun need not, in principle, add to aggregate harm. The gun owner seems to be in a morally different position than the polluter. (One might revise the pollution comparison by arguing that the gun owner adds to the probability of harm by creating a risk that would not otherwise be present. I don't accept this version either, but I will delay discussing till it takes center stage in Chapter 6.)

Another way to deny (2) is to hold that gun ownership may not be *malum in se*, but it may yet be *malum prohibitum*.[21] In English words, the idea is that owning guns may not be wrong in itself, but that it could be wrong to violate a law criminalizing the ownership of guns. Compare with a standard proposed example of *malum prohibitum*: Suppose there is a law against driving with a .04 blood alcohol content. Suppose also that you have had a drink and that your blood alcohol content is .06, but that you know you can drive safely. (I'm assuming you know this, and so it really is true that you can drive safely.) It might be that there are still good reasons to have a law at the lower threshold, as it may be that many people could not drive safely at that level of impairment. Perhaps it is wrong to violate the law and drive, even if it would be safe and therefore permissible to drive in the absence of the law. Analogously, one might argue that even if gun ownership would be safe (and so, permissible) in the absence of the law, it may still be wrong to own a gun in the presence of the law.

I'm skeptical that there are any genuine cases of *malum prohibitum*. But granting that premise, gun ownership seems meaningfully different. The idea of the drunk driving case is that there is some amount of drinking that is wrong, and the law exploits vagueness about the boundary. There is some amount of consumption that definitely makes driving wrong. But in the case of guns, it is unclear what could play the role of drinking. One might use a gun everyday while abiding norms of safety in each case. There doesn't seem to be any threshold amount of something after which gun use would be wrong, unless one imagines one to be using the gun in an unsafe way. There is no reason to think that gun ownership or use is, in itself, unsafe.

At this point, I think there is good reason to accept both premises (1) and (2), and to infer that criminalizing gun ownership violates the right not to be punished. Earlier, I suggested this was an especially important right. Before concluding this section, I want to underscore what would be interesting about the argument, should it succeed. If criminalizing guns violates the right against punishment, then prohibitions on various firearms may be seriously objectionable, even if the right to own a gun is not very important, or even if there is no right to own a gun at all. Compare with the right to doughnuts. Husak explains:

> When persons become subject to punishment – as is the case when any criminal law is enacted – more important interests are at stake than the liberty to perform whatever conduct has been proscribed . . . Suppose the state decides to curb the problem of obesity by criminalizing the consumption of doughnuts. If we assume that the liberty to eat doughnuts is not especially valuable, the state should need only a minimal reason to dissuade people from doing so. Clearly, the fact that doughnuts are unhealthy provides such a reason. This reason might justify noncriminal means to discourage consumption . . . But the interests implicated by a criminal law against eating doughnuts are much more significant. Persons not only have an interest

in eating doughnuts but also have an interest in not being punished if and when they disregard that proscription. This latter interest is far more important than the former, and qualifies as a right. Even though the state may have good enough reason to discourage the consumption of doughnuts, it may lack a good enough reason to subject those who persist in this conduct to the hard treatment and censure inherent in punishment.[22]

This is a long passage, but it repays careful attention. One might plausibly say, "What's the big deal about eating doughnuts — there's no right to a doughnut! Public health is more important." Even if this is all true, it doesn't follow that using the criminal law to prohibit doughnuts wouldn't implicate a very serious moral interest. Even if I have no right to eat a doughnut, the state may still violate my rights by prohibiting doughnuts.

Likewise, imagine someone who is unmoved by the defenses of a deontological right to gun ownership as presented in this chapter's earlier sections. Like the imagined doughnut regulator, the skeptic says, "What's the big deal about guns — it's just a way for some people to recreate. There's no right to guns. Public health is more important." We now are in position to issue an analogous response. Even if — contrary to my own view — there is no important right to own a gun, using criminal law to prohibit gun ownership violates a centrally important moral right: the right not to be wrongly punished. If the defender of gun control wants to argue public health is more important than that, they have more work ahead of them.

4. CONCLUSION

This chapter argued for gun rights in two ways. First, if one accepts something like Rawlsian basic liberties, then the case for a basic liberty to gun ownership is just as good as many other basic liberties. So there is a liberty-based case for a right to own guns. However, even if gun ownership is morally trivial, it is still wrong to criminalize it. So there is a right to own guns just because it is wrong for the state to criminalize gun ownership.

5

What Are the Effects of Gun Ownership in America?

What are the real-world consequences of privately owned fire-arms in the United States? Like everything else about the gun debate in America, trying to figure out the effects of firearm ownership for American society is intensely polarizing. This shouldn't be surprising. When a topic is politically charged, people form beliefs about it that favor their own political side. This is true even for relatively simple matters of empirical fact. If your side is in power, you think the economy must be doing well. If the other side is in power, you think the economy must be getting worse. Political partisans hate dissonant infor-mation. Even those of us who think of ourselves as educated and philosophically sophisticated often form our beliefs in a biased way. Though we may not realize it, our reasoning is often motivated by an aim of confirming or supporting our prior commitments.

For as long as philosophers have been arguing about guns, they've been appealing to the empirical literature about the social consequences of firearms. Pro-gun philosophers tend to favor empirical scholars who believe that guns are good for society – or what's often called the "more guns, less crime" hypothesis.[1] By contrast, proponents of gun control tend to see pro-gun empirical scholars as more biased and less trust-worthy than their opponents.[2] I am not suggesting that phi-losophers on either side are being disingenuous. But I want

DOI: 10.4324/9781003434818-6

to suggest an alternative approach to the empirical literature. Rather than trying to distinguish which side is right in a given empirical debate, a safer bet is for philosophers to think of themselves as outsiders. An outsider to a debate need not assess the competing arguments. Instead, outsiders can proceed by apportioning their beliefs to the beliefs of experts in the field. If most of the experts are on one side rather than another, we can be relatively more confident of the side with the greater consensus.

There are a few advantages to this strategy. First, it dispenses with the need to become expert enough in another field. Economists, criminologists, and other social scientists work for years to acquire the skills in their respective fields – just as philosophers do in theirs. (The extensive, recently updated analysis of the literature by the RAND Corporation offers a helpful overview.[3]) It isn't reasonable to expect that we can make up that ground just by reading through a series of studies. Second, it helps us manage our own biases. I admit that as a reader, I am always hoping to spot errors in the academic work of proponents of gun control. But that impulse isn't helping me get a fair assessment of what the world is like. If philosophers are like other sophisticated agents with political beliefs, we can suspect that this bias exists on both sides. We are all human. Third, if we can get clear on a relatively less controversial understanding of the empirical literature on guns, that can help us narrow in on our differences. As long as our empirical beliefs remain a source of controversy, that will obscure normative differences between advocates of gun rights and proponents of gun control.

This chapter will aim to set out some central findings about guns in a way that flags, but does not resolve, disagreements within the empirical literature. In the next chapter, I will try to make sense of the normative options they present.

1. ASSAULT WEAPONS

Deadly, high-profile mass shootings have focused political attention on how to curtail these high-fatality events. On October 1, 2017, the deadliest mass shooting in US history occurred at a music festival in Las Vegas. Firing more than 1,000 rounds from a hotel room overlooking the festival in only ten minutes, the shooter killed sixty people and wounded more than 400 more. A little more than a year later, the deadliest shooting at a high school in US history occurred. A shooter killed 17 people and wounded another 17 at a high school in Parkland, Florida. These events pushed mass shootings – and the associated concern with assault weapons – to the top of the national gun regulation agenda, so it makes sense to start here.

Mass shootings command great public attention. However, most mass shootings are not like those that get the most news coverage. Around 70% of mass shootings involve a shooter taking lives of members of his own family.[4] The rate of mass shootings has been roughly constant since the 1990s, but they have become more deadly.[5]

Aside from high profile mass shootings, another reason to focus on assault weapons is their increasing prevalence throughout American society. After declining slightly in the 1990s, firearm production has increased significantly since the early 2000s, and by the early 2010s there were more than 10 million firearms produced annually for US gun owners. The largest increases in production were in heavy caliber firearms and in concealable weapons.[6] Because the total number of cases is very small, it's hard to draw reliable inferences, but some estimates suggest that assault type weapons are used in more than half of mass murders, and that their use in these events is increasing.[7]

Would banning assault weapons help solve the problem? Empirical findings on assault weapons bans are mixed. Some find that the federal assault weapons ban had little effect, with number and fatality of mass shootings staying roughly constant.[8] Even some scholars sympathetic to gun control measures take a skeptical stance toward assault weapons bans. One observer holds that mass shootings "might provide a rationale for banning large capacity magazines and clips, but not for banning a smattering of semiautomatic assault weapon models that are functionally indistinguishable from hundreds of other semiautomatic models."[9]

Others do connect assault weapons bans with reductions in mass shootings.[10] However these results also underscore the small magnitude of the effect. Mark Gius gives 2012 as an example: in that year there were 12,765 murders, 322 using a rifle, 72 from mass shooting, and of those – just 30 using a rifle.[11] The point is that the total number of incidents impacted by an assault weapons ban (which would prohibit only a subset of rifles), is small both in absolute terms and as a class within gun crimes more generally.

Given the small absolute number of incidents, it may not be surprising that several authors fail to find evidence that assault weapons bans reduce mass shootings,[12] or observe any relationship between rates of gun ownership and rates of mass shootings.[13] Here is a simple explanation. While people perceive assault weapons as especially dangerous, there is no deep difference between them and other rifles. Assault weapons may have "bayonet lugs, flash suppressors, and grenade launchers," but they don't actually fire heavier or higher velocity rounds than other rifles. What makes them especially dangerous is their pairing with high-capacity magazines.[14] Another possibility is that the null result on assault weapons bans might be explained by the fact that compared with large capacity magazines (used in more than two thirds of instances), relatively few mass shootings involve assault weapons (around a quarter).[15]

Why think that large capacity magazines would make mass shooting more deadly? For one thing, if a shooter has a larger magazine, then they can shoot more rounds more quickly, and that may increase the density of their pattern. If shooters are placing more rounds into an area, then it's more likely that victims will be hit with more than one round, and multiple-impact injuries make it more likely that victims will die.[16] A second mechanism has to do with group behavior in active shooter scenarios. If there are pauses during which the shooter is reloading, switching out magazines, or changing guns, then there are opportunities for individuals either to seek cover or to disrupt the shooter. Large capacity magazines reduce these options by eliminating pauses in fire.

Do the data fit this theory? It's hard to say for sure, because the total number of events is so small. Some scholars estimate that between 1990 and 2017, nearly two thirds of high-fatality mass shootings (those with at least six deaths) involved large capacity magazines.[17] Over that period, there were a total of 69 high fatality shootings in the United States.

Do legal prohibitions of large capacity magazines help? Some scholars doubt that either bans on assault weapons or bans on large capacity magazines will save any lives. Kleck (2016) doubts that large capacity magazines are frequently used, and also doubts theory that explains how a ban could save lives. He finds that in all the mass shootings in which large capacity magazines were used, the shooter either had multiple magazines or multiple firearms, and so did not rely on magazine size for maintaining a high rate of fire.[18]

Other results suggest that bans on large capacity magazines could make a difference. In states with bans, more than half (55%) of high fatality shootings involved large capacity magazines. But in states without bans, 81% used them.[19] In several studies, the total number of victims (including killed and wounded) is around 60% greater when a shooter uses large capacity magazines.[20] Again, the numbers are quite small. This means that rather than between four or five deaths, there are seven to ten deaths. In general, these studies are looking at around 150–170 incidents (with four or more persons killed) between 2009 and 2017 or 2018.

2. CROSS NATIONAL COMPARISONS

Besides experiments with assault weapons bans at the federal and state levels in the United States, other countries have also responded to mass shootings by prohibiting guns. By far the most famous and widely studied of these is Australia's 1996 National Firearms Agreement, which banned automatic and semiautomatic rifles and semiautomatic and pump shotguns. The NFA was passed immediately in the wake of Australia's most deadly mass shooting, at Port Arthur. Its reach was expansive. On pain of becoming a felon, anyone who owned one of these guns had to sell it back to the government, resulting in some 650,000 legally owned guns being seized and destroyed.

This kind of sweeping action is much more dramatic than could be envisioned in the United States – at least anytime in the foreseeable future. The Australian case is important from a research perspective for precisely this reason. If the theory is that reductions in firearms per capita would reduce access to weapons, and that less access to weapons would mean fewer deaths, then we should most clearly see that theory working when guns are most dramatically reduced. In short, if we see results from gun control anywhere, we should see them here.

So what happened in Australia? As the theory would predict, homicides and suicides both went down. In the twenty years before Port Arthur, there were thirteen mass shootings. Since the bill was passed, Australia has only had one. But as before, those are not large numbers to work with, and studying the Australian case is further complicated by the fact that homicides were already declining when the bill was passed. Some studies find a statistically significant connection between the passage of the law and the reduction in mass shootings.[21] Several other studies have found especially dramatic consequences for suicides – perhaps including 80% reduction in suicide deaths.[22] A Vox article celebrates the Australian experiment with the headline, "Australia Confiscated 650,000 guns. Murders and Suicides plummeted."[23] The text of the article, however, is careful to note that whether the reduction in murderers was caused by the ban is a bit of an open question. Still, the author is optimistic that the reduction in suicides can be causally tied to the NFA. Other studies have extended these results from gun deaths to other gun crimes, especially armed robbery.[24]

Other researchers are more skeptical. Gilmour et al. observe that some earlier studies omitted to consider whether there might be trade-offs with non-gun suicides.[25] In other words, maybe there were dramatic reductions in the use of guns for suicide, but corresponding increases in other means. They find that after the NFA was passed, non-gun suicides did begin to increase, but (using a difference in difference model) find no statistically significant effect on firearm suicides. The authors also note that there were a variety of other anti-suicide strategies introduced in the 1990s, and they contend that their study is the first to use methods that "enabled us to separate these broad effects from the specific effects of firearms policy and shows that any changes in this single suicide method were likely not attributable to the NFA."[26]

It gets even more complicated. Suppose it is true that the Australian laws weren't actually the cause of the dramatic reductions in suicides and homicides from the 1990s on. Would that reveal that gun laws are ineffectual at saving lives? Skeptics about gun control think so. But other scholars advise greater caution.[27] It might be that strict gun laws do make a difference, but even before the '96 ban Australian gun laws were already creating that result. After all, Australia has much tighter legislative controls on gun ownership than the United States – a trend going at least back to the 1970s.

3. CONCEALED CARRY

Another contentious front of the US gun debates concerns the effects of various laws on the concealed carry of handguns. Different states have very different policies, so there is a lot of variation within the United States in how easy it is to legally carry a concealed weapon. The most permissive policy, permitless carry (or "constitutional" or "unrestricted" carry) allows for handguns to be carried openly or concealed without a permit or license of any kind. Permitless carry is common in the most traditionally pro-gun states, such as Arizona, Idaho, Wyoming, the Dakotas, as well as in Maine, New Hampshire, and Vermont. The next most permissive policy is one in which the state "shall-issue" a permit for concealed carry, provided that the person applying meets some set of criteria – usually including passing a background check, attending a certification class, passing an exam, and paying a fee. Anyone who meets these qualifications is issued a permit. Next are "may-issue" jurisdictions, which include the qualifications of "shall-issue" jurisdictions, but allow the granting authority some discretion in whether to issue a permit even to applicants who meet the qualifications. In practice, some "may-issue" states function basically like "shall-issue" states. In others, applicants must show a "good cause" for which they need to carry a weapon. In the most restrictive "may-issue" areas (some states have different policies in different counties), meeting the "good cause" condition is very difficult, so in practice the areas do not issue permits at all. Restrictive "may-issue" states include New Jersey, Hawaii, and Maryland, as well as some counties in New York and California.

A catalyst for the contemporary debate about concealed carry was Lott and Mustard's (1997) provocative finding that between the late 1970s and early 1990s, states with shall-issue laws had lower crime rates than states that restricted carrying weapons.[28] The finding was widely touted by proponents of expansive gun rights, including by the NRA itself. Some more recent studies have found no relationship, or have connected right-to-carry laws with higher crime.[29]

It's also possible that the relationship between concealed carry laws and homicide rates has changed over time.[30] Before the 1990s, the demand for handguns was relatively modest. In more recent years, moving to more permissive carry laws may spike demand for handguns. So if – as other data suggest – it is generally true that having a handgun in one's home increases risks, then we should find that looser carry laws also predict greater risk. For example, in 2015, the homicide rate was 4.11/100,000 in states with shall-issue laws, and 3.41/100,000 in states with may-issue laws.[31] According to this view, it might be that permissive laws were associated with reduced crime in the past, but are now associated with increased crime.

However, some recent studies continue to find the opposing result. In 2012, Illinois's concealed carry ban was ruled unconstitutional, and in 2013 Illinois adopted a may-issue policy for permits. A subsequent study found that property crimes in Chicago decreased after the change.[32] A similar relation may hold for homicides. One recent study finds a 10% higher murder rate in states with more restrictive concealed carry laws.[33]

Another proposed explanation compares the *ex ante* policy with the *ex post* policy. The idea is that if a state switches to a shall-issue policy from a may-issue policy, then there may be no gains in deterrence.[34] However, states switching from no-issue to may-issue or shall-issue policies (such as Illinois, above) do get a benefit in crime reduction.[35]

Does the theorized mechanism make sense? In other words, given what we know about what people know about whether other people have guns, should we expect that deterrence is even possible? Fortunato (2015) uses a survey method to find that the public's beliefs about firearm density are not connected to concealed carry policies. Fortunato infers that this is bad news for the deterrence theory.[36] However, it shouldn't surprise us that the general public lacks accurate beliefs connecting gun policy to gun density. Most people have no reason to collect any information about these facts at all. What really matters for the deterrence mechanism to work is whether people who might commit crimes are sensitive to this information. Some research does suggest that prospective robbers do think about how likely it is that their potential victim will be armed.[37] One recent study exploits a natural experiment in disclosure of carry permit holders to find that burglaries increased in areas with fewer permit holders and decreased in areas with more permit holders.[38] So it makes sense that there is some real deterrent potential in the relationship between prospective criminals and their prospective victims. Maybe you can deter crime if criminals think you have a gun.

4. CAMPUS CARRY

A related issue concerns "gun-free zones," in which carrying a weapon is prohibited in some local area, such as a college campus. In the aftermath of a deadly shooting at Virginia Tech, there has been some shift favoring the "campus carry movement" within state legislatures. There are now some ten states that mandate guns be allowed on college campuses. In 18 states, discretion is left to the individual campuses to choose whether to allow guns. In the remaining states, guns are banned from the state's colleges. Homicide rates on campuses are far lower than the national average (.11 per 100,000 vs. 4.8 per 100,000), so generally college campuses are already quite safe.[39] Given that campus crime is relatively rare, it makes sense that most studies show campus carry laws have no effect on crime in either direction.[40] Although not especially surprising as an academic finding, this result is remarkable in context of the vociferous political debate around these laws. Gun advocates see concealed weapons as a way for students and faculty to protect themselves from the rising danger of mass shooting. Opponents of guns see these would-be defenders as the problem from which we need protection: members of a potentially dangerous subculture. The balance of evidence seems to favor tempering both of these views. Concealed carry is neither vindicated as a needed tool for defense, nor blamed as the problem. Both sides may even be making a similar error: attributing excessive risk to members of campus communities in the first place. The media salience of school shootings makes it feel like schools are in jeopardy, when in fact schools are relatively safe environments – and likely becoming even safer.

5. WAITING PERIODS

A waiting period is a legally created space between the time when an individual starts the process of buying a gun and the time when the individual actually acquires the gun. This space of time can be created in one of two ways: by legislatively enacted mandatory waiting periods, or as a side effect of having to navigate some bureaucratic hurdles (such as a passing a background check and acquiring a permit) in order to purchase a gun.

There is a good theoretical reason to be interested in waiting periods. A great deal of violence, homicides, and suicides appear to be taken on impulse. How do we know this? Social scientists have found that there are increases in domestic violence after home teams lose football games, and that violent movies can work as substitutes for actual violence.[41] The idea behind findings like these is that many violent crimes are not the product of steady intentions across time. Acts of violence are done in fits of anger, and if those emotions can subside in some way without committing a crime, then the crime may never be committed at all.

If violence is committed on impulse, perhaps the same is true for many gun crimes. On this theory, if a would-be assailant could be stopped from acquiring a gun for a few days, then they might never commit an act of violence they had decided on in the heat of the moment.

Social scientists have found a variety of ways to see if waiting periods might work in this way. One strategy is to look at states that have specifically implemented waiting periods. Another is to study the time when federal policy imposed a waiting period. A third strategy is to use local delays in the gun market as a natural experiment: compare areas with delays to similar areas without delays.

Each of these strategies has produced evidence that waiting periods do reduce both homicides and suicides. One study finds a demand spike for guns prompted by the Sandy Hook shooting and Barack Obama's reelection in 2012. In counties that experienced delays in the ability to purchase a gun, there was a relative 2% decrease in homicides, suggesting that if there had been similar delays everywhere in the country, that would have accounted for 200 fewer murders over that six-month period.[42] Another study looks at the years from 1990 to 1998, when the Federal Brady Act imposed a national waiting period by requiring background checks for gun purchases. Luca, Malhotra and Poliquin (2017) compare states for which this policy created a new waiting period with states that already had a waiting period in place. Their results are especially dramatic. They find that waiting periods cause a 17% reduction in gun homicides, or around 39 fewer homicides per year per state. (They also find 17 fewer suicides per state year).[43] These numbers might be overstating the result somewhat, but either way it seems like waiting periods make a meaningful difference.[44] Studies of specific states, focusing on the time before implementing a waiting period to the time after, find similar declines in both homicides and suicides.[45] It also appears that the waiting periods were doing the causal work, since non-gun homicides didn't change during the time studied.

As with other policies, not all authors are so optimistic. Some state level studies have found no connection between waiting periods and either homicides or suicides.[46] One study even finds that background checks were connected to increased firearm homicide. The author concludes, "At best, gun-related murders would not be affected by these expanded background checks, and, at worst, gun-related murders would increase after the implementation of private sales background checks."[47]

One possible explanation for diverging results is that the details of how a waiting period is enacted matter for its consequences on gun-related violence. When a background check is conducted during the waiting period, there can be a considerable amount of variation in how thorough the check is, when the firearm is released, whether the terms are complied with, and even what kinds of offenses count or don't count as prohibiting a sale.[48]

6. OVERVIEW OF THE EVIDENCE

The aim of this chapter has been to survey the empirical literature about some of the contested issues in the American gun debate. This book is obviously in favor of quite expansive gun rights, so I've accordingly tried to downplay evidence from the principal empirical defenders of the "more guns, less crime" thesis – most prominently including Gary Kleck and John Lott. This is not because I have any particular objection to their work. As I noted earlier, philosophical proponents of gun rights have largely appealed to the empirical claims by Kleck and Lott (among a few others). I've tried to avoid this practice, for two reasons. First, it's not a good way of persuading people. If you didn't already favor gun rights, then you will be apt to see these works as apologetic, and so to discount them (rightly or wrongly) as biased. In fact, this is how philosophers favoring gun control have handled the issue. Both sides of the philosophical debate have tended to help themselves to empirical premises favoring their conclusion.

To my mind, the more interesting question is about what to do if the empirical results make trouble for our favored philosophical views. Second, excluding empirical work clearly favoring gun rights helps counteract the biases one might expect in a book like this one. Of course, the reader should likely still take this precaution advisedly. We all want to see the world as fitting together in a coherent way. It's psychologically pleasing to imagine that our favored normative views will also just happen to be the ones that lead, empirically, to the best outcomes. But there is no reason to think this should be so – unless of course we simply understand what we ought to in terms of producing the greatest social good. However, if – as I've argued here – what we ought to do is respect the rights of others, then it's an open question what kind of world will be brought to pass as a result.

With these caveats in place, there are two kinds of questions we can ask about this evidence. The first is about how likely different possibilities are. Suppose for example that a reliable weather report says there's a 40% chance of rain tomorrow. If I ask you if it's going to rain, the most helpful thing to say is not "yes" or "no" but to just tell me the percentage chance. We can ask a similar question about gun policy. What is the percentage chance, given the evidence we have, that various restrictions on guns will reduce crimes or deaths? The second kind of question is about what the range of permissible beliefs is. I don't mean morally permissible beliefs. Instead, I mean beliefs that are not ruled out by the evidence.

First, what should we think is most likely to be true? With respect to assault weapons, the evidence is mixed, but it seems that most of the evidence does not suggest that bans on assault weapon type rifles will make much difference. For one thing, bans – at least those in the United States – that prohibit assault weapons would not affect other rifles with similar caliber, velocity, and rate of fire. The evidence is better that banning large capacity magazines could make a difference. Skeptics try to rebut these findings by arguing that shooters could simply switch magazines or guns, but this seems compatible with thinking that bans on large capacity magazines could still reduce deaths. It might only take a few seconds for other people to flee the scene, or to disarm the shooter. However, we probably shouldn't expect that bans on large capacity magazines will have a large effect on the total number of gun-related deaths. The percentage of gun deaths from mass shootings is very small, and most mass shootings are not the kind of anonymous, large density events we see on the news. Instead, they occur in domestic settings, where weapon and magazine size probably make less difference.

It's a commonplace among gun control advocates that the United States is exceptionally violent, and that there are many more guns in America than in comparable countries. Can we infer that extensive prohibitions would work in the United States as they have in other countries? Here the most discussed point of comparison is Australia, and there are two complications. First, although I think most of the evidence supports the conclusion that suicides and (probably) homicides were reduced by the Australian ban, some recent, sophisticated studies support neither, and propose alternative explanations for the declines. Second, it is very unclear what can be inferred from the Australian model about the United States.

To get a sense, Australia bought back more than half a million guns, which made up perhaps 20 percent of the total number of guns in the country. In the United States, there are better than a million AR-15s sold each year, and that amounts to a relatively small percentage of annual gun sales. In 2020 alone, 20 million guns were purchased in the United States. Obviously, the scale of gun ownership in America dwarfs Australia. Proponents of gun control might suggest there are more opportunities for gains by reducing the total number of guns. At the same time, meaningfully reducing access to guns in the United States might be much more logistically complicated. Moreover, a paradox of gun regulation in America is that the very policies designed to reduce access to guns can spur people to buy them in record numbers. And in general, supply side regulation gets complicated when the magnitude of the project gets unwieldy – a lesson American liberals are keen to recognize in drug and alcohol policy, but are more reluctant to acknowledge about guns.

What about concealed carry? Here again there is conflicting evidence, but I think the balance of evidence favors the view that there are gains in security from less restrictive policies. These gains may be limited to moves from the most restrictive policies to any one of several more liberal policies. All the same, there is quite good evidence for some crime deterrence – at least in local cases.

So what range of viewpoints are – very generally – rationally permissible? By "rationally permissible," I just mean they are within the purview of what someone could believe, provided they're broadly curious about the empirical evidence and not merely rummaging through the data to support their prior ideological commitments. Consider four characters who sometimes appear in politically charged gun debates.

(1) The Gun Nut. Affirms the "more guns is better" thesis in every domain: homes, schools, concealed carry weapons, etc. Opposes waiting periods and background checks. Believes that private weapons are needed to stop the specter of tyranny.

(2) The Seer of "Both Sides." Sees that there are a variety of conflicting empirical findings, and throws up their hands. Doubts that we can make any progress in figuring out the consequences of different policies. Both sides have their own views, and that's all there is to it.

(3) The Pluralist. Holds that guns may have public health advantages in some ways and drawbacks in others.

(4) The "Only-In-This-Country" Prohibitionist. Sees America as a kind of last refuge of barbarism that civilized countries have progressed past by abandoning most private uses of firearms.

Among these options, I regard the Gun Nut's as least plausible, followed closely by the "Only-In-This-Country" prohibitionist. It does not seem plausible to think that guns are always a public health advantage. Likewise, the prohibitionist's view I find to be too ideological to be motivated by the evidence alone. However, the prohibitionist could marshal at least some evidence that guns are a public health disadvantage in a variety of domains, and so is not beyond the purview of the evidence. I differ with the seer of "both sides," because I think this position is unduly skeptical about our ability to assess the evidence.

The position I think is best supported by the evidence is the pluralist's. This view may be psychologically unappealing, because it denies that the same political side is right about each of the relevant sub-issues. But to stress what is by now a familiar point, there was never any good reason to anticipate that guns would either *always* be helpful or else *always* be harmful. The best public health consequences may involve liberalizing gun regulation in some areas and greater restrictions in others. However, to emphasize another familiar point, there is also no guarantee that the best thing to do from a public health perspective is also the morally right thing to do. If persons have rights − as I believe they do − then sometimes the exercise of those rights may involve suboptimal outcomes. In the next chapter, I will take up the question of how to think about different policy options in light of the public health evidence that we have.

7. CONCLUSION

The empirical literature on guns complicates things for both sides of the philosophical debate. The complication for advocates of gun control is that the empirical literature is, I believe, much less obviously supportive of gun control measures than is widely assumed. In particular, there is good evidence that private gun ownership sometimes reduces crime. The evidence surrounding mass shootings and assault weapons is complicated and − in my view − ambiguous. At the same time, things are complicated for the defender of gun rights. Waiting periods are well supported, and restrictions on high-capacity magazines enjoy considerable support as well. My tentative conclusion is that it is a mistake to think about a single, unified relationship between guns and social outcomes. We should be wary of generalizations either condemning or valorizing the role of guns in American society from an empirical point of view.

6

Policy Prescriptions

A central aim of this book has been to argue that owning a gun is ok – that it is a morally acceptable thing to do. People who own guns and care about guns are not in the grip of some kind of moral mistake. So while my central aim has not been to persuade you about any particular set of policy recommendations, it is hard to avoid policy questions altogether. After all, if people could be persuaded that gun ownership could coexist with some set of regulations they might accept, that might help make the case that owning a gun is, itself, an ok thing to do.

The last chapter acknowledged that gun ownership creates risks, including risks of homicides, suicides, and serious injuries.[1] There is a coherent normative outlook which holds that we ought to adopt the policy measures that would minimize these outcomes. I'll call this outlook an *ethos of protection*. I believe the ethos of protection is morally mistaken, but I won't try to defeat it here. I will, however, suggest that its revisionist implications extend well beyond gun control. A society committed to an ethos of protection would look very different from the one we have now. It would invite a radical rethinking of the role of government in individuals' lives. Everything from smoking and alcohol consumption to dietary choices and the use of private automobiles might be candidates for legislative restriction.

DOI: 10.4324/9781003434818-7

Notwithstanding its revisionist implications, some people may still favor an ethos of protection. What would an alternative look like? As one possibility, I'll offer what I'll call an *ethos of responsibility*. Few political slogans are more reviled than "guns don't kill people; people kill people." Gun control advocates think this mantra contains an obvious error. I'm not so sure. Once we agree that we actually don't want the political state to adopt an ethos of protection, then we will have to admit that many individual choices leading to sub-optimal public health outcomes are not appropriate for state regulation. In short, if we don't want to accept the society of a consistently applied ethos of protection, then we should also reject most proposed gun control regulations.

What does that mean for regulatory reform about guns? I will propose a division of proposed reforms into three broad categories. First, I will suggest some reforms that even a strict libertarianism about rights – of the sort favored in this volume – would still allow. The second category will include reforms which, while not compatible with strict libertarianism, would still allow a life that includes the values broadly associated with gun ownership. The third set of reforms will be those that not only violate strict libertarianism, but would broadly undermine the values commonly associated with guns.

1. GUN POLITICS MAKES NO SENSE

Imagine trying to craft the worst possible legislative agenda for gun regulation. To do this, you would have to find policies that would make almost no difference to public health, but would directly undermine and obstruct the permissible actions of as many Americans as possible. It would fail to achieve the aims of an ethos of protection, but it would threaten the kind of local apocalypse of value described in earlier chapters. If one were trying to devise the maximally bad policy, an efficient strategy would be to target the most iconic firearms to that part of America that cares about guns, while leaving in place most all of the risks that firearms create. The simplest and most direct way to do that would be through banning the AR-15. As the last chapter reviewed, assault rifle bans are unlikely to yield much benefit on their own. At the same time, the AR-15 is the most popular rifle in America, with around 1.3 million annual sales. A ban on the AR-15 would thread the needle of providing little protection for that part of the country worried about gun deaths while doing as much as possible to infuriate that part of the country that cares about gun rights.

And yet, remarkably, a ban on the AR-15 continues to be a central piece of the Democratic Party's agenda on gun reform.[2] It is almost as if Democratic politicians, including President Joe Biden, are mostly just aiming to antagonize their opponents. Even left-leaning policy analysts can be baffled by these priorities. The Democratic plan would allow extant owners of newly banned models to keep their guns, but they would have to register them and pay a fee of $200. That may not sound like a lot, but keep in mind that many gun owners inherit rather than purchase their firearms, and for those with more extensive libraries, $200 per gun will add up fast. That makes the policy especially burdensome to lower income members of society – ostensibly those whose interests the Democratic Party is most concerned to protect. Kim Kelly makes the point effectively, writing in the *Washington Post*:

> Regardless of one's opinion on guns and gun control, it is obvious that this proposal will disproportionately impact poor and working-class communities. Those within those

communities who already own firearms would be robbed of their ability to protect themselves and their loved ones, while their wealthier counterparts would skate by on their piles of cash . . . Biden's plan falls into a long line of government efforts to disarm the working class while keeping the lanes clear for the privileged who can afford whatever legal curveballs are thrown their way . . . [T]erritorial weekend warriors who feel no accountability to the community, and show little regard for gun safety, are exactly the kind of people who shouldn't have guns. By contrast, leftist community firearm clubs invest serious time into training and safety education, carefully vet their members and work arm-in-arm with marginalized communities they are invited to protect. And yet under Biden's plan, the former are who will be able to afford to hold onto as much firepower as they desire, while the people they want to hurt will be left high and dry.[3]

The background political context makes these choices appear all the more extraordinary. In past decades, political division in the United States was largely drawn along regional lines, with the coasts and upper Midwest voting Democratic and the interior and South voting Republican. America is now more polarized than ever, but today the most obvious divide is between urban and rural voters. Even in traditional Republican strongholds, densely populated urban areas vote Democratic. And the rural parts of traditional Democratic states vote Republican. Those Americans most likely to be harmed by the Democratic proposal centrally include residents of inner cities who – as Kelly describes above – have recently turned to firearms in 2020 for community protection, and rural voters, who have longstanding traditions of firearm ownership. The former group represent a core Democratic constituency, and the latter a crucial group of potential swing voters, especially in Midwestern "rust-belt" states.

How can we make sense of gun politics? Political proponents of gun control in the United States like to characterize their favored policies as 'common sense,' while casting their opponents as politically motivated and indifferent to evidence. As should be clear by now, I don't think either characterization is right. Earlier I described how I thought that guns play a symbolic role for many gun owners. Given how politics presently divides all facets of American society (who we talk to; date; work with; live with, etc.), I think the best explanation is that gun control is a symbolic issue for the American left in a roughly symmetrical way to how gun rights are a symbolic issue on the American right. I interpret the Democratic guns plan not as a measured response to the research, but as a symbolic salvo against their ostensible enemies. It wouldn't take much to do better if we care about protecting public health, or if we care about rights. I'll consider these points of view in turn.

2. AN ETHOS OF PROTECTION

To try to understand how we got to this point, I want to introduce two very different points of view on AR-15s. Both are normatively freighted. What I am going to suggest is that the middle ground in the gun debate is difficult to occupy. If one favors policies that promote public health, it will lead toward a quite expansive ethos of protection. On the other hand, if one favors liberty to collective well-being, it will lead to a quite minimalist ethos of responsibility.

To begin, consider a critical opinion offered by Heather Sher, a radiologist in Florida who performed CT scans of victims in the Stoneman Douglas High School Shooting in Florida. Sher describes in detail how the damage caused by a bullet fired from an AR-15 is much greater than the damage caused by a similar bullet fired from a semiautomatic handgun. While she was accustomed to seeing bullets lacerate an organ, the higher velocity rifle rounds would destroy organs. Lower-velocity bullets move through the tissue, but high-velocity rounds from powerful rifles leave "a swath of damage that extends several inches from its path." Sher draws a clear moral implication from these descriptions:

> It's clear to me that the AR-15 and other high velocity weapons, especially outfitted with a high-capacity magazine, have no place in a civilian's gun cabinet. I have friends who own AR-15 rifles; they enjoy shooting them at target practice for sport and fervently defend their right to own them. But I cannot accept that their right to enjoy their hobby supersedes my right to send my children to school, a movie theater, or a concert and to know that they are safe.[4]

Sher is a health care provider with first-hand knowledge, and she is clearly a morally serious person. She gives a helpful articulation of a common argument among proponents of gun control. The argument grants that many people who want to own and use AR-15s are doing nothing wrong. More than that, their individual use of the weapon may not impose any risks on anyone. Still, it doesn't follow that they have a right to own the gun. Given the extreme seriousness of being shot by a high-powered rifle, a prospective victim of such a shooting has a stronger claim than the person who just wants to use a rifle for recreation. The implicit suggestion, as I read it, is that we ought to compare individuals on both sides of the dispute who have representative claims, and then craft policy in a way that favors the person with the stronger claim.

I'll get back to this idea in a moment. To follow this procedure, we will have to look at someone on the other side of the issue, from their own point of view. Megan Hill, of Nephi, Utah, purchased an AR-15 as an all-purpose gun. Like many other firearms enthusiasts, she was impressed by its modularity. Everything about the gun is customizable. She explains:

> We looked at the AR-15, and it was all in one package. You can target-shoot with it, protect yourself with it, hunt with it. Luckily we haven't had to use it for self-defense, but it's a comfort knowing that it's there to protect my children and my family.[5]

Hill also values the gun as someone who has taken up competitive target shooting. She explains, "It has given me a sense of myself again: I'm going to make this goal, I'm going to accomplish something." As I described in earlier chapters, I think guns are closely connected to sense of self for many shooters. For Hill, her central moral concern is the same as Sher's – the safety of her children. However, Hill takes this consideration to point in the opposite direction. It's not a reason to ban the gun, but a reason to have one.

Now the comparison is not between someone's child's safety and someone else's recreation, but instead between the safety of two separate children. No one's child has greater significance than anyone else's. Does that mean the claims are comparable in strength? To this the proponent of gun control will respond that it's exceedingly unlikely like that Hill will actually use her rifle to protect her children. However, it's also exceedingly unlikely that Sher's children will face any violent threats at school or at the movies. Schools are safer now than they've ever been. In the two decades since Columbine, 64 students have been killed at school, or on average three student deaths per year.[6] If one writer is making a mistake about base rates and risk, then they likely both are, and the error is likely the same. Americans generally believe crime is going up, when in reality both crime generally, and homicide in particular, have fallen by nearly 50% since the early 90s.[7] By far, neither school shootings nor home invasion are near the top of the list of risks to our safety we incur every day. But once one inflates these risks, then either the pro-gun or anti-gun reaction can make sense.

I'm skeptical that the proponent of gun control can get any traction by framing comparisons like these. For the argument to work, the gun control advocate needs a more extreme moral theory. Here is one way the advocate of gun control might respond:

> It's true that the risks of school shootings are very low, but there is good evidence that the overall risks associated with guns in society exceed the overall benefits. There will be more preventable deaths in total in a society with liberal gun policies than in a society with restrictive gun policies. So if we care about minimizing preventable deaths overall, then we should adopt restrictive gun policies.

According to this view – which I find implicit in a great deal of the public health literature's recommendations – the underlying moral imperative is to save as many lives as we can. This is the outlook I have described as the *ethos of protection*. I find it to be a completely coherent moral outlook. Human lives are precious, and it make sense to prevent pointless deaths when we can.

The question I want to press is about how far the defender of the ethos of protection will take their view. Although the total number of mass shootings has increased, the risk of dying in a mass shooting remains extremely low. For a point of comparison, if we take the most expansive estimates for how many mass shootings there are each year, the number would still be less than the number of highway deaths each year *over Memorial Day weekend alone*.[8] If we are really committed to the ethos of protection, why not say something about these automobile related deaths similar to the argument against AR-15s above. Why should someone else's freedom to use their automobile be more important than the death of a child who perished in an automobile accident? If we prohibited, or significantly restricted, travel in private automobiles over Memorial Day each year, many of these lives could be saved. Do we really think the liberty to recreate over a weekend is more important than another person's life?

Now, my opponent will say this is unfair, because we really do regulate cars more than we regulate guns. I differ with that, but let's concede the point for now. There's still a sense in which the argument for restricting travel on holiday weekends is even stronger than the argument for restricting private gun ownership. When we drive on congested roads at high speeds, we are meaningfully increasing the odds of an accident. By contrast, when Megan Hill (or any other, ordinarily responsible gun owner) takes her AR-15 out to the range for practice, she is not contributing to any meaningful increase in the risks imposed on others. Advisedly safe use of the gun is not compounding the risk to others in the same way that even advisedly safe use of a car is.

Perhaps this argument seems extreme to you, but I think it can be pressed further still. Alcohol use in the United States, as a sociological matter, is much deadlier than gun use. As David Bruckner has pointed out, the case for broad prohibitions on alcohol is at least as strong as the case for broad prohibitions on firearms.[9] There are around 40,000 gun-related deaths in America annually, and some scholars estimate that if all states adopted a mix of the most efficacious gun regulations, around 4,500 lives could be saved each year.[10] To be sure, this is an important finding from a public health standpoint. (Also, it's worth noting, as I will describe later in the chapter, that some of the best supported policies are also more or less compatible with a libertarian outlook about gun rights.) To compare, there are around 140,000 alcohol related deaths each year, with the average life reduction of 26 years.[11] There is good reason to think that this number could be reduced significantly by greater regulation. If all states adopted Utah's blood alcohol limits for driving (.05 g/dL rather than .08 g/dL), that alone would likely save 1790 lives every year.[12] And this is a relatively small change. In Japan, reducing the allowable blood alcohol limit even more dramatically, from .05 to .03, was associated with a 20% reduction in traffic deaths.[13] Japan achieved these gains in part through highly punitive policies on drinking and driving, where drinking one glass of beer before driving could result in a $5000 fine, revoked driver's license, and three years imprisonment.[14] And this is not even yet to talk about the alcohol related deaths that don't have to do with driving. (To compare, alcohol results in around 380 deaths per day in America, of which drunk driving accounts for 32.)

Social scientists wonder about why there isn't more movement for gun control in the United States. My point here is that the premises which would justify such a movement would almost certainly spill over to other domains. What about the missing movement for alcohol control? Cigarettes cause nearly half a million deaths every year. What about the movement to prohibit smoking? Distracted driving causes around 3000 deaths annually.[15] Does anyone believe their unregulated right to a cell phone is more important than the life a teenager killed by texting while driving?

To get a sense of just how far the ethos of protection, consistently applied, might go, let's focus just on the issue of suicides. While the number of gun homicides remain much lower than they were in the 1990s, gun suicides, which account for slightly more than half of gun deaths, have lately reached increased to historic highs.[16] We also know that most suicides are impulsive, and most survivors of suicide attempts do not die by suicide. This provides reason to think that if a person lacks the means to take their own life in the moment, there's a good chance that this could contribute to avoiding a death. As a result, the prospect of substantial reductions in suicides is often touted as an important benefit of gun control measures.

How should we think about suicide deaths in the gun control debate? Opponents of gun control will say that suicides are not like homicides. Although any human death is a tragedy, suicide is chosen by the person who dies. This difference matters to regulation, because it undermines the kind of argument considered in this section. Homicide victims may argue that the violation of their right to life is morally more important than restrictions on someone else's liberty, and so homicide (or a risk of homicide) counts a justification for limiting others' access to guns. However, if a person takes their own life, their rights have not been violated by someone else. Proponents of gun control respond to this objection by saying that given what we know, empirically, about suicide, the choice to die – particularly to take one's own life with a firearm – is usually not an autonomous choice. It is made on impulse, without really willing the consequence. It's hard to say what makes a choice autonomous, but the motivating idea is that an autonomous choice is made from within. It represents the judgement of an agent's true or deep self. (This can be filled in in a variety of ways, but the differences won't matter for now).

Let's now take for granted that if a choice is not autonomous, then it's an appropriate candidate for the political state's coercive regulation. That way, if we agree that suicides are (mostly) not autonomous, then it is appropriate for the state to intervene to remove access to handguns to prevent suicides. Such policies seem well advised with an ethos of protection. But as before, we might ask: Why stop there? Consider for example the 650,000 heart disease deaths in the United States annually. Of these, the CDC estimates that at least 200,000 are preventable.[17] If only we ate better, exercised more, and avoided unhealthy foods, we could prevent many of these deaths. And let's suppose – for the sake of the thought experiment – that many unhealthy living choices are relevantly nonautonomous. I resolve that I should stick to a healthy diet, but on impulse I stop by the drive through for a large McDonald's fries. I judge that I should exercise daily, but then I give in to watching TV. Many unhealthy choices do not reflect our all-things-considered, stable judgements about how we should live. And it's worth pointing out that "unhealthy choices" extend well beyond diet. Some religious practices may be bad for public health. Living in certain regions of the country creates public health risks, including for the incidence of suicide.

What is the difference between nonautonomous health choices and the nonautonomous choice to take one's own life? My conjecture is that there is no deep, principled division between these things. It's true that unhealthy choices contribute to one's death unintentionally and in small increments, but it is unclear why either of these should matter. If we are concerned about avoiding preventable deaths that result from nonautonomous behaviors, then it seems like the state might take an active interest in regulating health choices for the same reasons that putatively justify its active interest in curtailing suicides. If this extends to the penalization of the means leading to death in the one case, then — *mutatis mutandis* — it might just as easily penalize unhealthy, nonautonomous lifestyles.

The point of this section is simple. If the state is justified in curtailing liberties to minimize deaths, then it will make sense to restrict private access to firearms. However, the defender of gun control will then either have to accept that the same ethos justifying restrictions on firearms justifies an apparatus of paternalistic intervention in the lives of persons on a scale few have imagined, or else find some principled difference between interventions to curtail gun use and interventions of other kinds. One candidate for such a principled difference is that gun deaths are either rights violations (in the case of homicides) or else often nonautonomous (in the case of suicides). But that route looks unpromising. Many automotive and alcohol related deaths involve rights violations, and a wide swath of the preventable deaths from unhealthy choices are plausibly nonautonomous. Some philosophers may be content to bite the bullet and allow that the state can interfere with the lives of individuals in much more expansive ways than most people suppose. My own view is interfering paternalistically in the lives of other persons is deeply objectionable. I think the ethos of protection is misguided from a moral point of view.

Some others may be unsure. If one is at least undecided, it will be worth thinking about an alternative.

3. AN ETHOS OF RESPONSIBILITY

Earlier I defended what I called strict libertarianism about rights, which has three features:

(1) It is wrong to interfere with morally permissible exercises of liberty.
(2) If it is morally wrong to interfere with an exercise of liberty, then a state policy interfering with that exercise of liberty is unjust.
(3) The state should interfere to stop one person from violating another person's rights.

What kind of alternative ethos might strict libertarianism support? Heidi Rapach, another AR-15 owner, offers the following assessment of gun rights:

> If someone wants to do damage they're going to find a way. That doesn't mean gun rights themselves are the enemy. It's the person. It doesn't mean that all the people that own guns and use them properly have to suffer for that.[18]

The first of these claims, I think, is open to objection. It may well be that harms done with a firearm might not be done in some other way, were the firearm absent. We have good reason to think that at least for many gun related injuries and deaths, the presence of a gun does make a difference. Still, the second of Rapach's claims I find quite plausible. If we believe that lawful uses of firearms are morally permissible and even a valuable part of life (as I have argued we should), then strict libertarianism holds that it would be wrong to interfere with them, even if doing so would lead to better public health consequences overall. Persons have rights not to be interfered with, and honoring those rights will not always be optimal from a utilitarian point of view. This is a fact of political life.

None of this is to say that my ability to shoot an AR-15 is *more important* than the life a child. If I imagine somehow being able to turn in an AR-15 to somehow save the life a child, I would certainly do it. Likewise, if you could prevent a child's needless death by taking a staycation over Memorial Day rather than traveling, I'm sure you would. But the real world doesn't afford us choices like that. What we can choose instead – or at least, what the country can choose instead – is whether to coercively curtail the liberties of some people in order to, in expectation, save the lives of others. And this is not the same choice.

Strict libertarianism forbids making this kind of tradeoff. But as Heidi Rapach observes, that doesn't leave us powerless against those persons who violate other's rights with guns. What we can do is hold persons responsible for their treatment of others, and do our best to do this in ways that protect members of vulnerable groups.

It will help to make this more concrete. An ethos of responsibility does not mean we cannot make changes to *status quo* gun laws. Many proposed policy reforms are either compatible with, or would actively be favored by, strict libertarianism. Others would not be supported by strict libertarianism, but would be broadly compatible with maintaining and exercising gun rights. A final group of proposed reforms would threaten the values associated with this way of life. Making no effort to conceal my views, I will refer to these three tiers of proposed reforms, respectively, as *liberal*, *moderate*, and *illiberal*. But

I acknowledge mileage will vary depending on one's theoretical commitments.

Liberal Reforms

(1) INSTANT BACKGROUND CHECKS

Most mass shootings are against partners or family members of the shooter.[19] Many mass shooters have a history of violence. So it is not surprising that background checks can be effective. If background checks can be completed at the time of purchase, then they need not infringe on the rights of anyone who is morally entitled to possess a weapon. In this way, these policies are compatible with even strict libertarianism.

(2) RESTRICTIONS ON DOMESTIC VIOLENCE OFFENDERS

Nearly half of mass shootings are committed by people who are already legally prohibited from owning a gun. Prohibiting domestic violence offenders from possessing firearms could help protect those most at risk. The strict libertarian should favor these reforms, because they would defend the rights of a vulnerable group while not constraining any other agent's rights. The latter claim depends on the idea that by committing a violent crime, a person alienates their right to possess a firearm. There isn't space to defend this view here, but I think strict libertarians will find it intuitive. If you violate another agent's rights, then you are at least liable to those uses of force needed to stop you from further infringing on others' rights.

What would such reforms look like? In many places, offenders may be prohibited from purchasing guns, but are either not required to surrender the guns they may already have in their possession, or else the requirement to surrender lacks any enforcement. This is the "relinquishment gap." One study finds that if offenders are notified of when and where they must surrender any guns in their possession, intimate partner violence with firearms could be reduced by around 15%.[20] A related reform is to clarify the terms of when someone is prohibited from possessing a gun, and to expand prohibitions to all cases in which an agent has waived or alienated their right.

(3) NON-PATERNALISTIC SUICIDE PREVENTION LAWS

The largest share of gun deaths are suicides, representing nearly 60% of the total. Finding ways to prevent people from using guns to take their lives would be a way of reducing the total number of fatalities. A couple of states now have laws which allow individuals to privately add their own name to the FBI background check system so they cannot purchase a firearm. They may also voluntarily take their names off the list, although removing one's name involves a delay. A preliminary study of these proposals found them to be quite popular, with a third of respondents saying they would use such laws.[21] Related laws could also allow gun owners to temporarily relinquish guns, or empower others to make decisions about relinquishing guns. These laws could be actively supported by strict libertarianism, since they create new options for citizens without imposing penalties on existing options.

(4) IDENTIFYING AND DISARMING VIOLATORS

Most states lack systems to identify persons who have purchased guns, but have since become prohibited from purchasing further guns. There is no libertarian objection to systems designed to protect others' rights by catching disqualified purchasers. There are models for how these policies might be put in place more effectively.[22]

(5) DETECTING AND RESPONDING TO INFORMATION LEAKS

Mass shooters often communicate their plans – sometimes on public social media platforms – well in advance. Some shootings have likely been prevented by the timely uptake and response to this information. Criminologists think more could be done, however, to encourage public reporting, and also to train authorities in processing and responding effectively.[23]

(6) PERMISSIVE CARRY PERMIT POLICIES

As described in the last chapter, some research supports the suggestion that liberalizing carry regulations may help reduce crime. Even though this makes guns more available, the evidence makes it plausible that some such measures, at least, could contribute to public health goals. In principle, safety goals and liberty goals are not in tension, and areas like this suggest they may sometimes align. This could perhaps also make available more administrative resources for some of the proposals on this list that would require greater investment in personnel and time.

(7) "GUN FREE" EVENTS

Armed counter-protests at public events can escalate quickly into hostile exchanges, or even worse. If strict libertarians believe that assembling with firearms should be protected, they should similarly allow that some citizens may want to freely assemble without firearms. As Fredrick Vars and Ian Ayres suggest, "Such a reform would require nothing more than adding a check box for 'gun-free'; events to the special application forms that organizers fill out to obtain permits for marches, rallies, or other demonstrations."[24]

(8) SOME "GUN FREE" ZONES

Citizens may also want to exercise associative freedoms in ways that exclude guns. Here I part company with some pro-gun authors, who object to gun free zones as a violation of the right to self-defense. My own view is that libertarian defenses of association will entail rights to exclude weapons. I am happy to allow visitors to bring firearms to my home (and in fact I encourage it), but you are free to require that guns be left outside of your home. This is no violation of the personal right to a gun, just as your discretion over what is said in your home is no violation of others' speech rights. What, then, should we say about public spaces, such as government buildings or state schools or universities? Here I think the most liberal policy is one that grants each member of the relevant institutions a say in determining whether guns should be allowed there. Even though I would be happy for academic institutions to allow private carry, I recognize that I'm in the minority. Nearly 95% of university faculty and students oppose guns on campus. I may disagree with their reasons, but I don't think my disagreement gives me a right to exclude them from having just as much power over how members of the university associate together as I have.

Moderate Reforms

(1) PERMITS AND LICENSING

Permits to purchase or transport guns do constrain the liberties of gun owners, and the transaction costs associated with these logistical undertakings can sometimes be burdensome and confusing. The complexity of legal requirements may present obstacles for citizens from lower socioeconomic strata.[25]

(2) "RED FLAG" LAWS

These are laws that authorize temporarily disarming someone who is judged to display dangerous or threatening intentions. There may be cases in which threatening others is sufficient to alienate a right to possess firearms, which would make these laws compatible with strict libertarianism. However, one might also fear that if these orders can be decided by relatives or others, their discretion may not reliably track the moral facts.

(3) WAITING PERIODS

As surveyed in the last chapter, there is theoretical and empirical reason to think that waiting periods can curtail gun deaths. There is a constraint on liberty, but if this constraint only involves waiting to acquire a firearm, then adequate prior planning could make it broadly compatible with all of the values gun owners worry about.

(4) LIMITS ON MAGAZINE CAPACITY

Magazine size limits are controversial. As with waiting periods, there is a constraint, but gun owners are free to carry multiple magazines, so the constraint does not seriously jeopardize the values associated with gun use.

(5) CHILD-ACCESS PREVENTION LAWS

Laws restricting children's access to guns are found to be among the best supported by RAND's comprehensive survey of studies.[26] Paternalistic laws are easier to justify on liberal grounds toward actual children, whose capacities for autonomy may not be fully developed. Such laws may provide a way of improving public health without objectionably restricting gun rights.

Illiberal Reforms

(1) BANS ON HANDGUNS OR SEMIAUTOMATIC RIFLES AND SHOTGUNS

At least some elements of this model, famously applied in Australia, remain popular with gun control advocates in the United States. But expansive prohibitions infringe on liberty in ways that also threaten the values that gun users care about protecting.

(2) LIMITS ON PRIVATE OWNERSHIP OR STORAGE

Some philosophers think it would be acceptable if individuals had access to guns, but did not privately own them. However, privately owning a gun is central to many of the associated values, as the Introduction and Chapter 1 outlined.

(3) IMPOSITION OF FEES ON EXISTING GUN OWNERS

Fees on existing guns, especially if additive, can impose considerable financial burdens that fall disproportionately on poor gun owners. Gun possession does not signal that a gun owner has the relevant wealth to pay these fees. Firearms are frequently passed down within families or given as gifts.

4. CONCLUSION

This chapter has described two ways of thinking about gun policy, which I've called an ethos of protection and an ethos of responsibility. In general, I think there is a moral gulf dividing these outlooks, which may be a small part of the reason why the gun debate is so polarizing. But there is still some good news. Surveying the range of proposed regulatory reforms shows that there can still be considerable overlap between the strict libertarian and the advocate of public health. In fact, I think it has largely been underemphasized that some regulatory measures not only permissible by the libertarian's standards, but actively supported by the underlying principles. Gun rights are important because rights are generally important. I doubt there is any special class of liberties that matter more than any other. So libertarians should be just as concerned about the liberties of persons who want to associate without guns, and of the rights to bodily integrity of vulnerable persons. We should take all the steps we can to protect these rights without violating the rights of others.

7

Undermining the Neo-Republican Case Against Gun Rights

Here are two ways your freedom could be violated. First, you're walking down the street on a dark night, and a mugger appears in front of you. "Your money or your life!" the mugger demands. Before, you could keep your money and your life. The mugger takes away an option (and an important one, at that!). Thus, the mugger violates your freedom.

Second, imagine getting a new boss at work. Your boss watches your every move. If you do anything the slightest bit wrong, you know that your boss could fire you. As it happens, the new boss never interferes with you in any way. They might not even speak to you. Yet you feel like you *have to* do whatever it takes to make your boss like you. Before, you could – at least for the most part – do things how you wanted. Now you feel like you must make your boss happy. You act based on what the boss wants rather than what you want. The boss's just being there undermines your freedom.

These two examples – the mugger and the boss – correspond to two different ways of understanding freedom. One way to understand freedom is as noninterference. As long as the mugger doesn't interfere with you, you're free. The second way to understand freedom is as nondomination. The boss doesn't interfere with you, but the fact that nothing is stopping the boss from interfering with you still makes you unfree. Philosophers in the tradition of civic republicanism would say

DOI: 10.4324/9781003434818-8

that the boss is *dominating* you. To be unfree is to be subject to domination by others.[1]

Up till now, I've defended gun rights without thinking about the civic republican conception of freedom. In this chapter, I'm going to consider things from a republican point of view. (I will use the terms republican and neo-republican to refer to the tradition in philosophy that understands freedom as nondomination. This is not related to the Republican Party in contemporary US politics.)

Some philosophers think that the republican view of freedom poses a challenge for gun rights. The challenge goes like this. If everyone in a society owns guns, then anyone would be able to interfere with anyone else. Nothing would be stopping them, so they could interfere arbitrarily, on a whim. Even if they don't in fact interfere, they still could. And if someone could arbitrarily interfere with you to remove your freedom, that means they dominate you. So, a society where everyone owns guns is a society where we all dominate each other. This is the problem of *mutual domination*. Some republican philosophers have argued that this problem shows that there should be significant limits on gun rights, or even an outright ban on private ownership.[2]

My aim in this chapter will be to respond to this republican objection to gun rights. I believe that mutual gun ownership does not entail mutual domination. A few legal theorists have argued that second amendment rights can actually protect against domination.[3] I'll make an analogous, moral case for guns in the next chapter. For this chapter, my aim is just to show that guns don't *create* domination.

This chapter is in four sections. Section 1 overviews republican theory. Section 2 presents the neo-republican case against a right to individual gun ownership. Sections 3 and 4 dispute the claim that private gun ownership places citizens in a relation of mutual domination. Everyone can have guns and live together without dominating each other.

1.   REPUBLICAN THEORY

Neo-republicans think that what really matters is not so much what makes for a free *action*, but what makes you a free *person*. Being a free person, republicans believe, is not merely the sum of free actions. Rather, it is possible for a person's actions to be free of interference, and yet for the person performing those actions to be unfree. In the case of you and the new boss, every single action you take may be free of interference. The boss, unlike the mugger, never threatens you. Still, the new boss makes you less free as a person. For republicans, unfreedom results not from mere interference, but from the presence of another agent who could interfere at will, even if – in the actual case – they choose not to. The paradigm cases illustrating this point include a benevolent master and sexist marriage.[4] The benevolent master chooses not to interfere with any of the slave's choices. As a result, the slave enjoys noninterference. However, the master has discretion to interfere whenever they like, so the slave's freedom from interference is modally fragile. Because the slave is subject to another agent with the ability to interfere, the slave remains – for republicans – unfree. The slave suffers from domination.[5]

Next consider a wife in a sexist marriage. Like the benevolent master, her husband may withhold from interfering with her choices. However, suppose that sexist norms are encoded within the society's legal institutions, empowering him to interfere if he so chooses. She may be able to remain free of interference, for example by making sure to remain in his good graces.[6] However, republicans see such compelled servility as evincing unfreedom – even if it maintains the availability of one's options. If a person is free, they should be able to look anyone else in the eye as an equal. Pettit refers to this as the 'eyeball test.'[7]

Neo-republicans understand freedom as the absence of domination. Here is a more formal definition:

A is free to φ or not to φ to the extent that no B has the uncontrolled ability to interfere arbitrarily in A's choices.[8]

If A has reason to fear that some B could interfere, or feels compelled to display deference to B to ensure that B does not become disposed to interfere, this indicates that B has the uncontrolled ability to interfere. Should these conditions obtain, A cannot look B in the eye as an equal.

What's bad about domination is how it feels to be dominated. Domination can erode a person's sense of self-respect. It can demand assuming a posture of deference or servility toward someone else. The dominated person's own actions can thereby reinforce their sense of powerlessness. If you are dominated in a marriage or by a new boss at work, you would rightly "burn with resentment."[9] Removing domination carries a sense of deep relief. "Let me fail to be good at toadying to them; let me lose the cunning required to keep out of their way. None of this matters if I really enjoy non-domination."[10]

Republicanism says that a person is unfree if someone else could arbitrarily interfere with them. This leaves two questions. First, what does it mean to have the capacity to interfere with another person? And, what makes interference count as arbitrary? This will come up again, so I won't give full answers here. First, about capacities. To have a capacity, it has to be the case that you could actually interfere. That is, it must be a capacity you could actually exercise. If you tried to, you could.[11] About the second question: Interference is non-arbitrary when subject to suitable control. If you could interfere with me, but there are rules and procedures that effectively control or limit you from interfering, and I can use those rules and procedures to stop you, then I'm not dominated. Or in other words, an exercise of interference is arbitrary if it is not "reliably constrained by effective rules, procedures, or goals that are common knowledge to all persons or groups concerned."[12]

2. THE NEO-REPUBLICAN CASE AGAINST GUNS

Consider the following case.

> *Wild West.* Everyone in society is armed to the teeth. If you decided to, you could shoot any of your neighbors. However, any of them could shoot you as well. Suppose that whoever shoots first wins. No one has any unreciprocated power over another person, so there is no inequality in opportunities for interference. At the same time, however, individuals can interfere without being controlled.

Andreas Schmidt notices that this case is different in an important way from any of the others we've looked at so far. There is no inequality in the ability to interfere. Unlike the mugger or the boss, no one has any more power to interfere than anybody else. So Wild West displays an important kind of equality.

At the same time, it seems like there are no controls on anybody's ability to interfere. Schmidt has helpfully distinguished three species of control.[13] *Preventive control* is the power to stop another agent from interfering. In Wild West, everyone does have preventive control, because anyone could shoot first (and thereby stop someone else from interfering with them.)

Abortive control allows an agent to remove an existing constraint to their action. In Wild West, no one has abortive control, because no one can stop anyone else from shooting. *Responsive control* is the ability to respond to interference after it has happened (for example, by retaliating). There is also insufficient responsive control in Wild West, because if someone shoots you, you can't do anything (because you're dead). Schmidt infers that in Wild West, everyone (a) can interfere with anyone else, (b) the interference can be arbitrary, and (c) there are not sufficient ways of controlling the prospect of interference. As a result, everyone is dominating everyone else. The society suffers from *mutual domination*.

Now we can apply the lessons from Wild West to the issue of gun control. Schmidt introduces three possible distributions of firearms: *prohibition, unequal ownership,* and *equal ownership.*[14] In prohibition, private gun ownership is (mostly) illegal. In unequal ownership, all citizens have a right to private gun ownership, but only a few own guns. In equal ownership, every citizen has a right to own guns, and almost everyone does. In republican terms, Schmidt holds that unequal ownership fails to realize the value of nondomination, because the people with guns dominate the people without guns. The problem is that moving to equal ownership does not resolve things. The world of equal ownership resembles Wild West. Everyone can interfere with anyone else. Crucially, though, equality isn't enough to stop domination. My power to interfere is not enough to maintain my freedom. What I need is security in knowing *that other people won't interfere with me.* Equal ownership denies me this assurance.

On the other hand, consider the world of prohibition. In this world, the state (mostly) removes guns from citizens, so the means for interference are significantly curtailed. Schmidt acknowledges that if citizens have no weapons and the police do, there may be greater power inequalities in prohibition than in equal ownership. His response is that "when state power is sufficiently properly controlled and employed in a sufficiently just manner, a concern with power relations can justify certain power inequalities if those are necessary to remove mutual domination."[15] Because prohibition offers greater control over interference, it is preferable to both unequal ownership and equal ownership. Freedom is better protected if no one has guns. Thus, neo-republicanism is held to support the prohibition of personal firearms, or at least significant restrictions on their availability.

3. THE CONDITIONS OF MUTUAL DOMINATION

I will grant the conceptual possibility of mutual domination, but I will deny that equal possession of firearms brings it about. The present section will clarify an ambiguity about mutual domination. The next section will argue that once disambiguated, private gun ownership alone will not suffice for domination.

I will briefly lay out the overall structure of my objection before getting into the details. Neo-republicans believe your freedom is undermined by another's capacity to interfere with you arbitrarily. Section 1 flagged that specifying the relevant concept 'capacity' will prove troublesome. We're now in position to see how. Sometimes an agent has a capacity to interfere, but this capacity is modally fragile – that is, it arises from transient features of the world. In this section, I will distinguish between a *bare capacity* to interfere and what we might call a *robust capacity*. I will argue that if the neo-republican specifies the bare capacity for interference, then equal possession of firearms will constitute domination, but so will so many other things that the resulting view of freedom will be useless. The only way to keep republican freedom conceptually distinctive is to limit it by strengthening the robustness conditions on the concept 'capacity'. However, once we shift to an idea of robust capacities, then equal possession of firearms will no longer be sufficient for mutual domination.

That might have sounded a bit abstract. It will help to work with a more concrete case. Imagine again the case of the mugger. Only now, imagine that the mugger secretly follows you, but doesn't actually confront you and demand your money or your life. If the mugger trails you by twenty paces all along your walk, then it makes sense to say that the mugger could interfere with you. You are subject to domination. (Imagine discovering you were trailed all night by a would-be mugger. Even if nothing bad happened, it would still be reasonable to be scared.)

Now the question is: What is it about the mugger that dominates you? Is it just the fact that the mugger has a potential capacity to interfere? Suppose the mugger didn't even notice you. Maybe the mugger was taking a nap on the other side of town. A potential capacity is not enough for domination. Next, suppose the mugger is aware that he could interfere, but does not do so. Is the mugger dominating in this case? Dorothea Gadeke argues that he does not. If we say that the mugger dominates by having the capacity to interfere and being aware of that capacity, then the concept will have become "too broad to capture the social reality of domination."[16] In other words, it's not helpful to provide an account of domination where more or less everything counts as domination. That would fail to explain what feels so bad about being in the sexist marriage, or enslaved to a benevolent master, or subject to the whims of a new boss. On the other hand, if we restrict domination to cases in which the mugger actually does interfere, then we'll lose the central republican idea: that your freedom can be compromised even when no one interferes with you. The result is a dilemma in which domination is so common as to be uninteresting, or is so limited as to vanish away entirely. Both lose the concept's explanatory appeal.

What we need is a better account of the capacity to interfere – one that will help to distinguish when someone is dominating you from when they just happen to be around. To get at this, let's distinguish between the *bare capacity* to interfere and what we might call the *structurally constituted capacity* to interfere.[17] In the paradigm cases of domination, there were rules or legal or social structures that enabled one agent to dominate another. The master can interfere with the slave at will not only because he is aware of the slave and has the physical means to do so, but because his power has the backing of the state's legal rules. These institutions enable the master to interfere across a wide range of possible worlds, and so constitute his capacity to interfere as robust.

Something similar can be said for the sexist marriage case. Legal institutions – for example, coverture laws – may help give the husband power to interfere with the wife. Social structures can also entrench the husband's capacity for interference. In a host of informal ways, social norms can impair disadvantaged members of society from exerting control over others' interference. Such norms promote domination.

To see the idea, imagine a society where some people were arbitrarily given a special anti-mugging alarm. If they were threatened by a mugger, they could press a button on the alarm, and law enforcement would immediately be signaled. Other members of the society, let's suppose, don't get the alarm. (Maybe they don't have the right connections, or the alarms are only given to the rich and privileged. The exact details don't matter for now.) The mugger has the capacity to interfere with anyone. However, given the society's institutions, his capacity to interfere with those equipped with alarms is fragile. Others will come to their aid, use force to protect them, and will use the legal system to provide redress. By contrast, the mugger's capacity to interfere with those who lack alarms is robust. This shows that it is not the mugger's bare capacity to interfere that creates domination, nor is it the interfering action. Instead, it is the mugger's capacity as constituted in part by social or legal structures, which render that capacity robust against variation in how others (including the potential victim) respond. In other words, to have domination, the mugger must have the capacity to interfere, and the rules, institutions, and social norms of the society must make it hard to stop the mugger from exercising their capacity. Domination is promoted by the *structurally constituted capacity* to interfere.

There's one other way we could specify the concept of domination. Imagine a case in which there is no single mugger who can overpower any other person walking through the park, but there are groups of people who – collectively – could overpower any particular individual. Do the potential groups constitute a dominating power in virtue of their potential to interfere?[18] The problem here is closely related to the mugger's dilemma. If the group is dominating, then it seems like any set of people who could together overpower an individual imposes domination, which enlarges the concept too much. On the other hand, if the group only dominates by actual interference, then the core conceptual innovation is squandered. We should deny that the group's potential for domination constitutes actual domination.[19] The potentially dominating group lacks the relevant agential features. Even if each person wants to exercise power over the same individual, they may not know that they share the same desires. They must also coordinate with each other about how and when to act together. In short, they must be organized in a way to share intentions together. Without the requisite coordination, they lack even an "episodic kind" of group will.[20] On this second strategy, domination is made robust through a kind of intentional activity. Groups of people who could potentially dominate do not thereby count as dominating. Only when they have coordinated with each other to form and maintain the relevant intentions do they dominate the potential victim. Domination requires the capacity to interfere, plus some kind of *intentional monitoring* with a conditional aim to interfere.

To recap, just having the bare capacity to interfere is not enough to dominate another person. Saying otherwise would create a dilemma for republican views of freedom. So republicans should say that we have to add something to the bare capacity for interference. One thing we could add is a structurally constituted capacity to interfere. That is, we could say that the boss/master/mugger dominates you when their capacity to interfere is made more robust through legal rules or social norms. Second, we could say that boss/master/mugger dominates you when they are engaged in a kind of intentional monitoring activity that could sometimes result in their aiming to interfere.

4. UNDERMINING THE NEO-REPUBLICAN CASE FOR PROHIBITION

We now have the resources to revisit the world of equal possession of firearms. Does equal possession produce mutual domination? I believe it does not.

First, equal possession of firearms alone does not produce legal rules or social structures that facilitate domination.

Consider some of the common ways in which structures could constitute domination.

(a) *Legal Asymmetries in Power*: Are some citizens legally entitled to perform some actions, or hold others accountable for actions, in ways unavailable to other citizens?

(b) *Social Structures*: Are some citizens' claims informally regarded as more important or morally urgent than those of others? Are violations of the rights of some less likely to be remediated?

(c) *Language Structures*: Does the society lack concepts to appreciate forms of wrongdoing to which some members are particularly vulnerable? Are the speech acts of some members undermined or silenced by dominant modes of interpretation?

All we know about the world of equal possession of firearms is that everyone has a gun. That tells us nothing about how the legal system works, whether there are asymmetries of legal power, whether social norms privilege some citizens at the expense of others, or if linguistic practices give some groups more power than others. Everyone owning a gun is not enough for structurally constituted domination. It is enough for a bare capacity to interfere with others, but as we've seen, even the neo-republican should deny that this is enough for domination.

The same can be said about *intentional monitoring*. In the world of equal possession, it is not clear that any agent has an actual capacity to interfere with you. Imagine a mugger who has forgotten they have a gun in their backpack, or who hasn't even noticed a prospective victim walking on the other side of the park. Such cases preclude domination because the capacity to dominate goes un-actualized. The mugger lacks the intentional profile needed to dominate. Likewise, the world of equal possession need not be one in which agents intentionally identify and monitor prospective targets of interference. Just because everybody has a gun, it doesn't follow that anyone is using it against anyone else, or thinking about using it, or making plans to use it, or anything like that. There might be a bare capacity to interfere, but that's all. And if the bare fact that one could interfere with a gun creates a world of mutual domination, then what about other tools with potential for interference? Anyone with a car could subject others to physical interference, and anyone with access to the internet could interfere with other persons in a variety of ways. If equal possession of firearms is enough for domination, then there are plenty of other technologies that could land us in a world of mutual domination even if there were no guns at all.

Where did the neo-republican argument for gun control go wrong? The argument suggested that responsive control was insufficient to blunt the force of domination. Even if it were possible to respond to someone who interfered with someone else, that was not enough to ensure, prospectively, that no one would interfere.

My suggestion, however, is that sometimes responsive (or abortive) control may also have a preventive aspect, when the anticipated mode of response is visible and publicly known. When these conditions are met, an exercise of control confers greater security against the threat of interference, thereby rendering prospective threats modally fragile. For example, it's common practice for homes with an alarm system to also have yard signs announcing that they have an alarm. If you have an alarm like this, then you can be confident that if the alarm is tripped, neighbors or authorities will come to your aid. The alarm provides a kind of responsive control that also creates an incentive – given the social and legal structures in place – for prospective burglars to leave you alone.

The alarm system is better than nothing, but it of course falls well short of complete control. For one thing, the alarm system offers responsive control, but it does not stop burglars from targeting your home. Nor does it abort their efforts. Although the alarm system is a form of responsive control, its advantage is in its publicly available meaning. Because the alarm system is visible, and because neighbors and police can be expected to act in support of its signal, it confers greater control over interference. In addition to providing *responsive control*, it also provides what we might call *deterrent control*. That is, its presence sends a signal to potential burglars that makes them less likely to interfere.

Let's return to the society where everybody has a gun. Equal possession of firearms falls short of mutual domination in three ways. First, equal possession is compatible with the absence of any intentional monitoring to interfere. Like the mugger who has forgotten he has a gun or fails to notice a prospective victim, gun owners may simply lack any plans to interfere. Second, equal possession may provide deterrent control, in which the public expectation of responsive control curtails the prospect of domination. Chapter 5 presented some evidence that guns do sometimes function like the alarm system. When would-be burglars are more aware that their victims may be armed, that reduces their interference. Third, equal possession may include social and legal structures that strengthen defenses against domination. In any case, the fact that everybody has a gun tells us nothing about whether the legal and social structures make domination possible, or work to prevent domination.

Equal possession of firearms is not sufficient for domination. There may be societies where everybody owns a gun and people are dominated by each other. But likewise, there could be societies where everybody owns a gun and yet people are mostly safe from domination. I don't think this is that surprising. There is no evidence that citizens of Wyoming – whose neighbors are almost certainly armed – feel dominated more than residents of New Jersey, where relatively few households have guns. In fact, something approaching the opposite is true. The sociology of rural gun ownership suggests that gun owners have strong positive affect toward fellow gun owners, and actively encourage others to adopt the practice of keeping guns in their homes.[21] There is an easy explanation for this: gun ownership is a significant source of shared identity, and a reliable proxy for a cluster of further shared identities.

On the other hand, imagine if equal possession alone was enough to create mutual domination. If that were true, we should expect citizens in situations approximating equal possession to be full of fear. Domination, after all, is the kind of thing that feels terrible to be subject to. Schmidt encourages this thought in suggesting that in equal ownership, citizens are effectively "thrown into intense power relationships with strangers."[22] If domination is present, they should feel continually 'under the thumb' of those dominating them. But this is not what we find. If an intense power relationship is present, we should see some evidence of it. This does not appear to be the case.

If these relations don't look like mutual domination, then what does? Schmidt's own motivating case is helpfully informative. He writes:

I recently watched footage of the 2017 Neo-Nazi rally in Charlottesville, Virginia. Some protesters were heavily armed and explained they were ready to use their weapons against anyone challenging their racist vision of the United States.[23]

Notice what this case adds to equal possession. For one thing, it describes not only armed citizens, but citizens who have armed themselves in an agency-sharing way. It is also clear that they robustly intend (and publicly announce their intentions) to interfere with people who don't share their racist beliefs. They also want to control social and legal structures – promoting their racist beliefs as part of a political agenda for the United States. Finally, their public displays are intended to expose the absence of any social or legal means to curtail their intimidation. In this way, their protest seeks to exploit and perpetuate conditions in which they can exercise interference against specific targets. This kind of case reveals a much richer set of conditions, which are also – importantly – exactly the further conditions necessary to distinguish real domination from the bare capacity to interfere. The case exhibits a structurally constituted capacity to interfere, and a shared intentional state aimed at robustly interfering.

There are plenty of cases in which people own guns around each other, but don't dominate each other. When we do start to worry about domination through private guns, it's not the guns that are doing it, but the way in which social and political activity aims to use guns to shape the social world. There's a lesson in these examples for everyone. Owning guns is not domination. But also, guns can be used by people seeking to dominate others. To paraphrase Jack Shaefer's *Shane*, a gun is as good or as bad as the person who uses it.

5.   CONCLUSION

This chapter has considered a neo-republican objection to guns. According to the objection, if everyone owns guns, then we all dominate each other, and so we are collectively less free. In this chapter, I've argued that the objection fails. For the concept of domination to be meaningful, domination must involve a robust capacity to interfere. Republicans have provided a couple of different ways in which a capacity can be robust. It might be structurally constituted, or it might be intentionally monitored. Mutual possession of guns does not, itself, create the structural conditions for domination. Neither does it show anything about the intentions of any agents. When republicans give cases in which gun ownership feels like domination, these cases tend to bring in additional features of intentionality or new structural conditions. So it is not surprising that there are plenty of societies where lots of people own guns, but don't experience mutual domination. Whether we all own guns and whether we live in a social world of republican freedom are separate questions.

8

Can Private Gun Ownership Protect Freedom?

Could the private ownership of firearms provide a resource for countering political domination? There is some precedent for an affirmative answer. James Madison wrote that "being armed" was an advantage Americans possessed "over the people of almost every other nation."[1] A few legal theorists have continued to see the second amendment – like other amendments – as part of a bulwark of civic freedom.[2]

For the most power, however, philosophers treat this question as unworthy of serious consideration.[3] The idea that private firearms could protect political freedom is derided in academic and popular media alike.[4] It just seems so implausible that individual persons could curb excesses in state power with private arms. The goliath of federal power, it seems, is too great for any private citizen to stand against. Any effort to place a thumb on the balance of relative power seems like the stuff of fantasy. Jeff McMahan writes, "Individuals with handguns are no match for a modern army."[5] Firmin DeBrabrander writes, "Tyrannical governments hardly fear rifles, and handguns, and even assault rifles in the hands of citizens."[6] And besides that, philosophers have scoffed at the thought that a modern liberal democracy could really exercise power in a tyrannical way. Jeff McMahan calls it a "delusion" and DeGrazia regards it as "not a realistic possibility."[7] DeBrabrander describes the thought

DOI: 10.4324/9781003434818-9

that "those in power are not to be trusted" as a "deep cynicism" harbored by the gun rights movement.[8]

There are three questions here. First, could the government of a liberal democratic society ever act in a dominating way? Second, is ever plausible to think that the private ownership of guns could constrain the political state's exercise of political power? And if so, third, is it ever plausible that the private ownership of guns could constrain political uses of power in ways that helped counter domination and thereby promote republican freedom?

My answers to these questions will be yes, yes, and yes. I believe the social science makes it clear that even liberal democratic regimes can act in dominating ways. I will take this claim up in section 1. More controversially, section 2 will suggest a way in which private firearms can constrain government power. I will focus on the case of the "Sagebrush Rebellion" – the armed opposition to the federal government by the Bundy family and their allies in the Nevada desert in 2014. To be very clear, I will not be arguing in defense of the Bundys' standoff. I will just be using the case to illustrate how privately owned arms can, in principle, modify government behavior. Section 3 will argue that the private possession of firearms can help curb domination, and so help protect freedom. I will focus on the civil rights movement. Qualitative and quantitative social science support the hypothesis that the possession of guns by civil rights activists helped protect its members from the threat of arbitrary power and violence. Section 4 will respond to an objection about whether any of this is realistic.

1. POLITICAL STATES AND DOMINATION

Neo-republicans have traditionally been quite optimistic about the political state as a means of countering domination. In this section, I will venture an opposing view. While the political state can help ensure conditions of nondomination, it can also – itself – be a dominating power. It would be a mistake to argue that the state must be either one or the other. Rather, given its administrative vastness and heterogeneous consequences for differing population groups, the state can be both a source of nondomination and a dominating power. Looking at the state in a generalized, monolithic way can obscure its potential for domination.

My suggestion that the state can be a threat to republican freedom is nothing new. Modern era republicans were frequently concerned with the state's potential for dominating power. Madison's praise for Americans almost unique position as an armed people was not out of nowhere. The seventeenth century English republican theorist, James Harrington, had held that to maintain the value of independence, yeoman property owners also had to bear arms.[9] These citizens could provide protection against tyranny threatened by foreign sources or from within one's own political society. The anti-federalist *Federal Farmer* likewise regarded it as important that "the whole body of people possess arms, and be taught alike, especially when young, how to use them."[10] This early republican thought was that to be on equal terms – to pass the 'eyeball test' of equality – it was sometimes important to bear arms.[11]

In more recent times, neo-republicans have thought of the state as part of the solution to domination rather than part of the problem. Neo-republicans have traditionally held that justice requires a political state. If the state didn't exist, we would be morally required to create it.[12] But given the state's extensive and unified power, doesn't it present an obvious threat of domination? Not necessarily, according to Pettit. Following the historical republican tradition, Pettit avers that constitutions can limit state domination.[13] A constitutional state can curtail private domination while its constitution prevents the state itself from becoming a source of domination. If some agent wants to dispute the state's judgment resolving a conflict between private actors, then that agent can challenge the state, itself, through constitutionally specified procedures. It can thereby "encounter the authority, under a balance-of-power scenario, just as an agency for defending others against interference," and not as a hierarchical power in that particular context.[14] The two parties can meet each other as equals, and the eyeball test can be satisfied with a private citizen being able to look the state (in its guise as an artificial person) in the eye.

Pettit hopefully conjectures that it's "not entirely outlandish" to think that political states might accommodate themselves to constitutional constraints along these lines.[15] The claim is intended as a general articulation of republican governance. But the devil is in the details. Consider, for example, a particular protest movement – the summer protests in 2020. Political and law-enforcement authorities were perceived as betraying deep unwillingness to accommodate procedures of mutual accountability. Protests erupted specifically in response to acts of apparent arbitrary power. Some enforcement tactics seemed perhaps intended to inflict harm in unpredictable ways. For example, the use of police dogs – more extensive in some cities than others – resulted in potentially life altering injuries to nonviolent protestors, including persons who were not suspected of any crimes.[16] The response by authorities also actively signaled that no form of control would be available to citizens or media. Protestors were picked up and detained by federal officers in unmarked vans.[17] Officers displayed no identifying information and refused to provide their names or badge numbers.[18] Municipal officials and some national political leaders tried to alter this practice, but their halting success exposed deep difficulties in holding the state accountable, even under intense political scrutiny.

Let's leave aside the details of the protest movement. What is important, for present purposes, is the question of how to think about these incidents in terms of republican values. The kinds of policing practices that the protests brought to public attention were mostly already known within the academic literature. The expansion of police powers, catalyzed by "law and order" political campaigns, had been underway in American society for decades.[19] Additional funding, favorable court rulings, and ordinances criminalizing an expanding array of behaviors have granted police officers greater discretion and expanded available tactics.[20] These tactics had been deployed within urban, Black communities. Such practices mostly stayed below the radar of national media. Still, some scholars suggest that the legalized subjugation of minority communities amounts to a "racial authoritarianism" within broader democratic society in the United States.[21]

Authoritarianism may sound like a strong label, but republican theory advises otherwise. The central issue is that members of urban, minority communities perceive themselves as vulnerable to enforcement without – crucially – any recourse to constitutional protection. In a qualitative study of Black community members' knowledge of law enforcement, Weaver, Prowse and Piston find that traditional concepts are inadequate to explain the gap between these their experiences and standard democratic practice. They explain:

> [W]hen residents of highly policed communities say "it may not be written policy, but that's what they do," they

are providing crucial counterknowledge of governance based on concrete, firsthand experience. When they say "The laws aren't for us" or "that may be your reality but it isn't ours," or "we're not in the constitution," they are not mounting a challenge that their preferences are not registered (a common concern in our subfield of late). Instead, they are demanding a revision of the state as operating in antidemocratic ways as a matter of unofficial policy in their neighborhoods.[22]

The problem described here, as the authors note, contrasts sharply with boilerplate concerns about electoral minorities. The issue is not that the system fails to represent their views, but that it excludes them entirely. Their complaint echoes republican concerns. If some people are effectively "left out" of the state, then the constitution does not effectively limit how the government interacts with them. They cannot turn to any other apparatus within the state to encounter enforcement authorities as merely another agent, tasked with a particular job within the state's broader architecture. Instead, the institutions exempt authorities from responsibility for constitutional violations.[23] The frequently unofficial status of such policies further undermines accountability.

When the political state imposes domination, republicans should expect that this will feel like a restriction on the freedom of those under its control. And in fact, this is what we find. I've offered only the briefest overview here, but one qualitative study of Black youth in Chicago offers an illustrative finding, which is that those interviewed were skeptical of claims that the United States ensured protection of rights to everyone, even while acknowledging that there was a sense in which citizens did have important rights. One respondent summed up the contradictions, "[B]ut in the United States, to me it seems 50/50. Like you're free but then again you're not."[24] It would be at least tempting for citizens confronted by a seemingly hostile state that the system was "not only closed to them but out to get them."[25]

In short, the political state enjoys a vast capacity for interference with individual persons, which has expanded in recent years due to political change and technological advances. Enforcement officials likewise enjoy considerable discretion in deciding when and how to interfere – especially within vulnerable, minority communities. The absence of constitutional constraint borders, at the limit, on authoritarian. All of this helps underscore the unique dominating potential of the state. As the last chapter discussed, domination is created not through possession of weapons alone, but through an extensive set of social and legal norms. The fact that such power is locally employed in limited areas may conceal state domination from public view, but its lack of salience does reduce its seriousness for those subject to it.

2.   PRIVATE FIREARMS AND GOVERNMENT ACTION

In this section I will take up the question: Can citizens with guns make a difference to what the government does? In April, 2014, the Bundy family initiated an armed confrontation against federal authorities from the Bureau of Land Management.[26] The Bundys had originally held a grazing permit, but after their grazing rights had expired in the 1990s, Cliven Bundy had refused to sign a more limited agreement and in the following years accrued over \$1 million in fees. On April 5, the BLM – perhaps under pressure from the prospect of environmental lawsuit – issued an emergency closure of the federal land and began rounding up the Bundys' some 900 cattle, with the intention to later auction them. Cliven Bundy, along with his sons Ammon and Ryan, responded by calling for help from ranchers across the West. Soon hundreds of protestors, including militia members, joined the Bundys. Following a tense standoff between armed federal agents and armed protestors, the BLM abandoned its operation on April 12.

The Bundys and their supporters declared victory, but the BLM had only said it would work to resolve the issue through the courts. Nearly two years later, the government charged all three of the Bundys with conspiracy and assault. At issue was whether they had tried to enlist gunmen to force government agents to discontinue rounding up the ranch's cattle. At the trial, Ryan Bundy represented himself, and alleged in his opening statement that government snipers and surveillance cameras had been positioned around his family's home prior to their call for armed supporters. It seemed, at best, an unlikely allegation, drawing mockery in media and academic circles. However, in December 2017, U.S. District Judge Gloria Navarro dismissed the charges and declared a mistrial. As one reporter observed contemporaneously, claims of government misconduct, "dismissed by the government as fiction by paranoid anti-government activists, have largely turned out to be true. And it's taken the government nearly two years, and three trials, to admit as much."[27]

How did this happen, when the government's case had appeared so strong? A government whistleblower memo alleged that the BLM had seriously mishandled the case, and that agents overseeing the cattle roundup had mocked and displayed prejudice against the Bundys, their supporters, and their religion.[28] In a subsequent defense of her finding, Navarro reaffirmed the importance of the government's failures to make the relevant disclosures to the defense. The decision referenced the insertion of snipers and camera surveillance around the Bundy home as evidence of provocation:

> The Government's theory of prosecution relies on the fact that the Defendants were acting offensively instead of defensively. The evidence that the Government failed to disclose would have assisted Defendants in showing that the officers were engaging in provocative conduct and the Defendants were not the aggressors. Therefore, the undisclosed evidence might have supported a theory of self-defense.[29]

The case was dismissed because the court found that the government withheld evidence that agents had engaged in provocative conduct, and that individuals had a limited right to self-defense triggered by an officer's "bad faith or provocative conduct."

How does this bear on republicanism and rights to firearms? As noted above, my aim here is not to suggest that the Bundys' refusal to abide federal grazing laws was justified. Moreover, commentators have agreed that there is no constitutional case in their favor. The issue, instead, revolves around whether the Bundys and their supporters were able to constrain an exercise of arbitrary state power through their use of firearms. And here, there is – at least – a case. The Bundys believed that the government was disposed to act outside of legitimate procedures, in a dominating way. And in fact, the court's finding suggests some plausibility for this view, both in how the government acted and in its subsequent nondisclosure. One might counter that the government's violations occurred before the Bundys' call for armed resistance, and so their use of private arms was irrelevant to their eventual victory. That response calls for examining the relevant counter-factual: Would the government have used surveillance, force, and snipers in the ways that it did, were it not for their prior knowledge of the Bundys' possession of private firearms?

This issue can't be settled here. My point is just to illustrate that it is premature to think that private firearms cannot check arbitrary exercises of state power on the grounds that private groups lack the requisite force to effectively confront armed government officers. This is because private actors may be able to use firearms against the state in a way that qualifies as self-defense, or – at least – in a way that comes near enough to so qualifying that other agents of the state will play their constitutional role in constraining state interference. The use of individual firearms, in other words, may be part of a more complex set of actions, which jointly exercise abortive control (stopping state interference) and responsive control (counter-manding prior excesses in state force).

One final point is worth mentioning in connection with the Bundys and republicanism. After the federal state came to his timely aid, Ammon Bundy subsequently parted ways with the Patriot Movement to support the rights of immigrants, including undocumented immigrants, and also later publicly endorsed the Black Lives Matter movement. In both cases – having been the beneficiary of constitutionally sanctioned control over arbitrary power – Bundy's rationales struck a republican tone. He had been persuaded that members of these groups were subject to robust threats of interference, and likewise deserved protection.

3. PRIVATE FIREARMS AND REPUBLICAN FREEDOM

Can private guns help protect freedom? In this section I argue that they can, focusing on the civil rights movement.

Even before the concept Black Power was introduced in 1966, armed self-defense figured into the civil rights movement in meaningful ways.[30] In 1964–65, Black war veterans formed defense organizations out of "pragmatic necessity."[31] With government protection often absent, armed groups engaged in a variety of activities from protecting protest movements to rescuing individuals from Klan attacks. One such group was the Deacons for Defense, who provided armed defense escorts for nonviolent protestors at segregated cafes, as well as for the military veteran James Meredith's march across Mississippi. Meredith had intended to demonstrate that white supremacists lacked power to intimidate Blacks from registering to vote. Early in his march, Meredith was shot in the back and seriously injured.[32] The Deacons also guarded the homes of Black leaders after the violent murder of a Black Deputy Sheriff, O'Neal Moore, in Bogalusa, Mississippi.

In other quarters, members of the civil rights movement were uncomfortable with the Deacons' show of force, in part fearing its repercussions within White media outlets. Henry Austin, the group's public relations director, responded that the civil rights movement wasn't addressed to "blacks in the ghetto, the ones who are trapped."[33] Statements like this one are clearly intelligible in republican terms. Austin is not objecting to the civil rights movement, but speaking on behalf of those who have no means of controlling the arbitrary power threatened against them.

At times, leaders in the movement invoked the republican tradition of the founders directly, seeing themselves as the inheritors of the American Revolution's principles. Issues of *The Black Panther* quoted from Patrick Henry, and in addition to weapons, members of the group carried copies of the Bill of Rights.[34]

How important were firearms to the civil rights movement? On one level, firearms had a clear, pragmatic function. In times and places where the political state did not afford protection from armed members of a hostile majority, having an armed defense made sense. During vulnerable periods, many NAACP leaders in Mississippi were armed, or relied on armed guards for protection. They did not begin by carrying weapons, but armed themselves in response to violent reprisals against other forms of action.[35] Likewise, armed night patrols were seen as helping curb white vigilante violence.[36] Once protection from law enforcement became more reliable – starting in 1967 – groups like the Deacons became less active. It may be difficult, in this context, to separate the efficacy of firearms from the movement generally, as there was no strict separation between unarmed and armed protests. Instead, the use of armed self-defense provided protection and support for prominently vulnerable groups.

Was carrying firearms instrumental to curtailing domination? Remarkably, there is good evidence for the efficacy of guns in protecting citizens against private and state-sanctioned dominating forces. Economists have exploited variation in firearms restrictions in the Jim Crow South to investigate whether greater access to guns by Black citizens helped curb White violence. Makowsky and Warren find that in states and years when Black citizens had greater access to firearms, there were fewer lynchings. They report, "This correlation opens the door to the possibility of firearms serving an important role in self-defense in a poorly institutionalized state."[37] Of course, it's difficult to untangle causation, because it might be that the same states with racially motivated firearms restrictions also placed Black populations at greater risk of racist violence. Makowsky and Warren investigate by looking at

White law enforcement and handgun restrictive legislation. They find that greater White law-enforcement predicts lower Black access to guns, and that in years when Black citizens had reduced access to guns, there were more lynchings.[38] In short, anecdotal accounts about members of the civil rights movement protecting their communities with firearms are empirically supported. As one leader in the movement observed, "the showing of a weapon stops many things."[39]

On another level, being armed carried a kind of symbolic import. Besides seeing themselves in the tradition of the founders, guns provided a "symbol of defiance."[40] They afforded a source of pride to protestors who could see themselves as willing to defend their communities. Firearms bolstered self-respect for members and signaled commitment to sympathetic outsiders and adversaries alike. Some philosophers are skeptical about the moral significance of symbolic values, but symbols are connected to our sense of meaning over time, which is something over which persons have a deep moral interest.[41] Aside from the moral import of such symbols, armed self-defense aimed at providing "psychological conditioning" to deepen members' commitment and encourage others to join. It may also have incited additional White resistance, so in consequentialist terms the record may be mixed. My purpose here is not to argue that all uses of firearms were efficacious in promoting nondomination, but that there were mechanisms through which they could make a positive difference. My suggestion is that as both a direct instrument of self-defense and a broader symbolic marker of resistance, firearms contributed to resisting domination.[42]

4. GUN RIGHTS AND NON-IDEAL REPUBLICANISM

The political state can pose a significant threat of arbitrary power. The state's capacities to exercise power over persons greatly exceed those of any private person or group. The state can also use this power in an arbitrary way. So the state poses a risk of domination. Private gun rights can help counteract domination, either through direct use or possession, through their symbolic import, or through catalyzing the conditions for securing control over state power through other agents – including other parts of the state, itself. So private gun ownership can help promote the value of nondomination.

Before concluding, I will consider an important objection to this line of reasoning, which I'll call the *asymmetry objection*. The objector I have in mind argues as follows:

> I grant that the state may be a dominating power, and that in exceptional cases private firearms may either help limit domination, or may at least be part of a broader suite of causal forces limiting state domination. However, this conclusion is heavily stylized by the particular cases considered. The cases selected include extreme examples of state domination, and highly favorable portrayals of private firearms. So the state is presented in a non-ideal way, while private actors are idealized. This unfairly prejudices the result in favor of private exercises of power.

I call this the asymmetry objection because it points to an asymmetrical presentation of the political state and private actors. The argument describes how in the real world, the state can act very badly. On the other hand, it offers an in-principle defense of private firearms, with a mere couple of empirical cases clearly selected for their favorable coding.

To some extent, my response to this objection is to admit guilt as charged. However, my core aim in this section will be to contend that republican proponents of state power are likewise guilty of the opposing asymmetry: idealizing the state while considering private actors' real-world deficiencies.

To make this point, I will return to Schmidt's republican argument for gun control from the previous chapter. Schmidt considers that private firearms might offer a kind of control over the prospect of interference, but responds with an empirically minded rebuttal: "Numbers suggest firearms are only rarely successfully used in self-defense."[43] This claim opens an ongoing controversy among philosophers and the empirical scientists to whom they appeal. I've discussed this controversy already in Chapters 5 and 6. My purpose here is just to suggest that pointing to the small number of successful cases is an odd line of rebuttal for a republican theory. Compare with the right to sue for breach of contract. It would be strange to observe that as an empirical matter, there are only a small number of suits brought to court, and thereby to infer that the right to sue for breach of contract offers little value in controlling interference by other agents. Republicanism furnishes precisely the resources needed to explain why the number of cases isn't what matters. What matters is whether one can robustly control another's arbitrary interference. The robustness condition signals the relevance of nearby possible worlds. In other words, what matters is that, in the event of a breach of contract by your employer, you robustly possess the right to bring a case. The mutual, publicly accessible knowledge of such a right might help explain why there are relatively few breaches, and correspondingly few accusations of breaches.

Defenders of gun rights say something analogous about the small number of defensive uses of firearms. It's at least possible that the benefits accrued from possession are largely a result of the robust possibility of defensive use. Furthermore, these benefits may well be describable in republican terms. One might have security in knowing that one could defensively use a firearm, and thereby benefit from the corresponding control over interference, without "using" it in the narrower sense of brandishing or discharging.[44] This repurposes the republican's point about marriage and coverture law: what matters for securing nondomination is that the woman *could* exercise legal rights, rather than the *number* of such exercises.

The republican case against gun rights appeals to empirical deficiencies in private ownership, which departs from a world of ideal practice of private control over interference. On the other hand, the republican case appeals to an idealized picture of state control over interference. The final footnote in Schmidt's paper presents this in a helpfully clear way. It reads in part:

> [S]ometimes gun ownership might be considered necessary to prevent a government from accruing dominating power over all its citizens (rather than just one group) . . . Republicans can in principle allow that widespread gun ownership can be necessary to respond to domination in very particular settings. But considering mutual domination, this should only apply in cases of drastic institutional failure. A functioning republican constitution, democracy, criminal justice system, and international political system would obviate the need for widespread gun ownership.[45]

In this passage, the world in which private gun ownership could helpfully counter domination is regarded as likely ruled out on the grounds that the political state will do its job well. Private non-domination is made to seem unlikely by being described as available in only "very particular" conditions. But these suppositions are just made by way of assumption. This point is acknowledged by Schmidt, who grants that his essay remains "within the realm of 'somewhat ideal theory.'"[46] The problem, I am claiming, is that the part of the essay in ideal theory is in how it anticipates the political state will act, and the part not in ideal theory pertains to how private ownership will work. So it is then not surprising that we should find the well-functioning, constitutionally constrained republican state will serve republican values better than real-life private actors.

Whether the state or private actors more closely resemble their idealized counterparts is an empirical issue, plain and simple. This chapter has aimed to show that in the real world of a deficient republican state, there are at least a few real-world cases in which private ownership can contribute to republican values. Another fair way to proceed would be by setting out an idealized regime of private ownership and comparing it against an idealized regime of constitutional state control. For now, I will settle for the more limited conclusion that a republican case for gun ownership is locally possible given some combination of state and private circumstances. Given widespread skepticism about the value of private guns as a tool against political tyranny, this is, itself, a substantive conclusion.

5. CONCLUSION

The argument of this chapter is that private firearms may help counter domination, including state domination. To recap: risks of domination can lurk even with liberal democratic states; the private possession of firearms can change how governments act; and sometimes the private possession of firearms can help realize republican freedom. Exactly how far this argument can be extended is a matter for further investigation. For now, I select cases only to provide evidence of the possibility. However, in my view this is sufficient to show that the derision of philosophers toward this thesis is unjustified. The civil rights movement furnishes the most compelling example. Not only is it not crazy to think that private gun ownership could sometimes help protect against political domination – it seems very plausible that there is at least one such case in the United States' history.

It is ok to own a gun – in two different ways. First, it is ok in the sense that it is within one's sphere of personal rights. This right is important to self-defense, but it is also important as part of having the personal liberties to live a meaningful life of one's own choosing. Second, it is ok in the sense that it is morally acceptable. There is nothing morally wrong with owning a gun. These are two different claims because our political rights include a host of things we morally ought not do – rights to use speech in ways hurtful to others, to associate in ways that exclude or express contempt, and so on.

This latter point raises a question that I will end on. Suppose it is true that there is a right to own a gun. How can that right be exercised without any moral reproach? Here I think it is important to recall that the case I've made for gun rights focuses on the way in which a relatively very small slice of American society values guns. For the vast majority of people, guns will never play the role I've suggested they play for those few people who really care about them. The case for gun rights depends on appreciating values most people will never share. So it is for most values in a liberal society. We protect certain liberties we (mostly) don't care about, because a few people – perhaps people we neither understand nor care to understand – do.

Conclusion

165

DOI: 10.4324/9781003434818-10

As a defender of gun rights, I think this is an important thing for me to keep in mind. If people who care about guns want their own small-minority values to be protected, we should remember that and want the same for values we don't share. Just as gun rights are a difficult case for people who hate guns, people who love guns will likely be challenged by the rights of people who hate them. But of course, their values are just as good as ours or anyone's. So we do well to remember that in a society that protects gun rights, we also need to protect the rights of people who fear guns, want to avoid them, and even build identities around disapproving of them. All of those values are morally acceptable, too. For gun rights to be exercised without any moral reproach, we need to ensure that everyone can pursue their morally acceptable values. It shouldn't matter whether we share those values, are indifferent to them, or revile them. Respecting other people means letting them make their own choices. And respect for other persons is what morality fundamentally asks of us.

Notes

INTRODUCTION

1. Michael Huemer, "Is There a Right to Own a Gun?" *Social Theory and Practice* 29, no. 2 (May 1, 2003): 297–324, doi: 10.5840/soctheorpract 200329215.

2. Jennifer Robison, "Decades of Drug Use: Data From the '60s and '70s." Gallup.com, July 2, 2002, https://news.gallup.com/poll/6331/Deca des-Drug-Use-Data-From-60s-70s.aspx.

1

1. David DeGrazia and Lester H. Hunt, *Debating Gun Control: How Much Regulation Do We Need?*, 1st edition (New York: Oxford University Press, 2016), 180.

2. DeGrazia and Hunt, 187.

3. DeGrazia and Hunt, 9.

4. DeGrazia and Hunt, 8.

5. I've anonymized the names throughout.

6. Jeff Spross, "How Obama Diagnosed Trumpism Way Back in 2008." *The Week*, accessed August 28, 2022, https://theweek.com/articles/ 610945/how-obama-diagnosed-trumpism-way-back-2008. The full quotation was widely reported at the time and continues to be discussed as a diagnosis for Trumpism in rustbelt America.

7. Robert A. Orsi, *History and Presence*, Reprint edition (Cambridge, MA and London: Belknap Press: An Imprint of Harvard University Press, 2018), 91.

8. Orsi, 109.

9. Cf. Katherine J. Cramer, *The Politics of Resentment: Rural Consciousness in Wisconsin and the Rise of Scott Walker*, Illustrated edition (Chicago, IL and London: University of Chicago Press, 2016).

10. Seana Valentine Shiffrin, "Promising, Intimate Relationships, and Conventionalism." *The Philosophical Review* 117, no. 4 (October 1, 2008): 481–524, doi: 10.1215/00318108–2008–014.

11. Shiffrin, 508.

12. Samuel Scheffler, *Equality and Tradition: Questions of Value in Moral and Political Theory*, 1st edition (New York and Oxford: Oxford University Press, 2012).

13. F. Carson Mencken and Paul Froese, "Gun Culture in Action." *Social Problems* 66, no. 1 (February 1, 2019): 3–27, doi: 10.1093/socpro/spx040.

14. Jennifer Carlson, *Citizen-Protectors: The Everyday Politics of Guns in an Age of Decline* (Oxford and New York: Oxford University Press, 2018), Chapter 2.

15. Katarzyna Celinska, "Individualism and Collectivism in America: The Case of Gun Ownership and Attitudes toward Gun Control." *Sociological Perspectives* 50, no. 2 (June 2007): 229–247, doi: 10.1525/sop.2007.50.2.229; Bindu Kalesan et al., "Gun Ownership and Social Gun Culture." *Injury Prevention* 22, no. 3 (June 2016): 216–220, doi: 10.1136/injuryprev-2015–041586.

16. Dennis Vicencio Blanco, "The Gun Control Debate: Why Experience and Culture Matters." *International Journal of Public Administration* 39, no. 8 (July 2, 2016): 628, doi: 10.1080/01900692.2015.1028639.

17. Kellie R. Lynch, Tk Logan, and Dylan B. Jackson, "'People Will Bury Their Guns before They Surrender Them': Implementing Domestic Violence Gun Control in Rural, Appalachian versus Urban Communities: Appalachian Domestic Violence Gun Control." *Rural Sociology* 83, no. 2 (June 2018): 333, doi: 10.1111/ruso.12206.

18. Ryan W. Davis, "Symbolic Values." *Journal of the American Philosophical Association* 5, no. 4 (2019): 449–467, doi: 10.1017/apa.2019.25.

19. Christine M. Korsgaard, "Two Distinctions in Goodness." *The Philosophical Review* 92, no. 2 (1983): 169–195, doi: 10.2307/2184924; Christine M. Korsgaard, *Creating the Kingdom of Ends* (Cambridge: Cambridge University Press, 1996), doi: 10.1017/CBO9781139174503.

20. Elizabeth N. Simas, Scott Clifford, and Justin H. Kirkland, "How Empathic Concern Fuels Political Polarization." *American Political Science Review* 114, no. 1 (February 2020): 258–269, doi: 10.1017/S0003055419000534.

Why It's OK to Own a Gun

2

1. Jonathan Lear, *Radical Hope: Ethics in the Face of Cultural Devastation* (Cambridge, MA and London: Harvard University Press, 2008), 2.

2. Lear, 35–36.

3. Lear, 38.

4. Lear, 49.

5. Lear, 32.

6. For an overview, see Allen R. McConnell, "The Multiple Self-Aspects Framework: Self-Concept Representation and Its Implications." *Personality and Social Psychology Review* 15, no. 1 (February 1, 2011): 3–27, doi: 10.1177/1088868310371101.

7. I discuss this in Davis, "Symbolic Values."

8. Mencken and Froese, "Gun Culture in Action"; See also Carlson, *Citizen-Protectors*.

9. Andrea C. Westlund, "Selflessness and Responsibility for Self: Is Deference Compatible with Autonomy?" *The Philosophical Review* 112, no. 4 (2003): 483–523.

10. Hugh LaFollette, *In Defense of Gun Control* (New York: Oxford University Press, 2018), 90.

11. Samuel Arnold, "The Difference Principle at Work." *Journal of Political Philosophy* 20, no. 1 (2012): 94, doi: 10.1111/j.1467–9760.2010.00393.x.

12. Martin O'Neill, "What Should Egalitarians Believe?" *Philosophy & Public Affairs* 36, no. 2 (2008): 119–156, doi: 10.1111/j.1088–4963.2008.00130.x.

13. Gerben A van Kleef and Jens Lange, "How Hierarchy Shapes Our Emotional Lives: Effects of Power and Status on Emotional Experience, Expression, and Responsiveness." *Current Opinion in Psychology*, Power, Status and Hierarchy, 33 (June 1, 2020): 148–153, doi: 10.1016/j. copsyc.2019.07.009.

14. Julie L. Rose, *Free Time* (Princeton, NJ and Oxford: Princeton University Press, 2016).

15. See G. A. Cohen, "The Structure of Proletarian Unfreedom." *Philosophy & Public Affairs* 12, no. 1 (1983): 3–33.

16. van Kleef and Lange, "How Hierarchy Shapes Our Emotional Lives."

17. Orsi, *History and Presence*.

18. Immanuel Kant, *Critique Of Judgement, The* (South Bend, UNITED STATES: Infomotions, Inc., 2000), 62, http://ebookcentral.proquest.com/lib/byu/detail.action?docID=3314533; See discussion in Sandra Shapshay,

"At Once Tiny and Huge: How Philosophers Describe the Feeling We Call 'Sublime.'" Text, Scroll.in (https://scroll.in), accessed September 28, 2022, https://scroll.in/article/904615/at-once-tiny-and-huge-how-philosophers-describe-the-feeling-we-call-sublime.

19. Shapshay, "At Once Tiny and Huge."

20. Shapshay.

21. Shapshay considers the psychology of ambivalence. Sandra Shapshay, "A Two-Tiered Theory of the Sublime." *The British Journal of Aesthetics* 61, no. 2 (April 1, 2021): 123–143, doi: 10.1093/aesthj/ayaa047.

22. Joshua Martela and Frank Hicks, "A New Dimension to a Meaningful Life." *Scientific American*, accessed September 28, 2022, https://www.scientificamerican.com/article/a-new-dimension-to-a-meaningful-life1/.

23. Huanhuan Zhao et al., "Relation Between Awe and Environmentalism: The Role of Social Dominance Orientation." *Frontiers in Psychology* 9 (2018), https://www.frontiersin.org/articles/10.3389/fpsyg.2018.02367.

3

1. John Locke, *Locke : Two Treatises of Government* (Cambridge, UK and New York: Cambridge University Press, 1988).

2. Huemer, "Is There a Right to Own a Gun?"; Michael Huemer, "Gun Rights as Deontic Constraints." *Social Theory and Practice* 45, no. 4 (November 1, 2019): 601–612, doi: 10.5840/soctheorpract20201375.

3. Huemer, "Gun Rights as Deontic Constraints," 605.

4. Jeff McMahan, "Why Gun 'Control' Is Not Enough." Opinionator, 1355940232, https://archive.nytimes.com/opinionator.blogs.nytimes.com/2012/12/19/why-gun-control-is-not-enough/; Ctd. in Dustin Crummett and Philip Swenson, "Gun Control, the Right to Self-Defense, and Reasonable Beneficence to All." *Ergo, an Open Access Journal of Philosophy* 6, no. 20201214 (October 16, 2019): 1039, doi: 10.3998/ergo.12405314.0006.036.

5. Huemer, "Gun Rights as Deontic Constraints," 604.

6. F. M. Kamm, *Intricate Ethics: Rights, Responsibilities, and Permissible Harm* (Oxford: Oxford University Press, 2008).

7. Huemer, "Gun Rights as Deontic Constraints," section 5.

8. Nathan E. Kruis et al., "Firearm Ownership, Defensive Gun Usage, and Support for Gun Control: Does Knowledge Matter?" *American Journal of Criminal Justice*, September 30, 2021, doi: 10.1007/s12103-021-09644-7.

9. Crummett and Swenson, "Gun Control, the Right to Self-Defense, and Reasonable Beneficence to All," 1040.

10. We assume that you cannot sacrifice yourself; you are not large enough to stop the trolley.

11. cf. Caspar Hare, "Should We Wish Well to All?" *The Philosophical Review* 125, no. 4 (October 1, 2016): 451–472, doi: 10.1215/00318108–3624764.

12. Crummett and Swenson, "Gun Control, the Right to Self-Defense, and Reasonable Beneficence to All."

13. Kieran Setiya, "Ignorance, Beneficence, and Rights." *Journal of Moral Philosophy* 17, no. 1 (February 19, 2020): 67, doi: 10.1163/17455243–20182841.

14. Crummett and Swenson, "Gun Control, the Right to Self-Defense, and Reasonable Beneficence to All," 1052.

4

1. Jason Brennan, "Against the Moral Powers Test of Basic Liberty." *European Journal of Philosophy* 28, no. 2 (2020): 493, doi: 10.1111/ejop.12497; Samuel Freeman, *Rawls* (Abingdon, UK and New York: Routledge, 2007), 46.

2. John Rawls, *A Theory of Justice* (Cambridge, MA: Harvard University Press, 2009), 3.

3. cf. John Tomasi, *Free Market Fairness* (Princeton, NJ: Princeton University Press, 2012), doi: 10.1515/9781400842391; Alan Patten, "Are The Economic Liberties Basic?" *Critical Review* 26, no. 3–4 (October 2, 2014): 362–374, doi: 10.1080/08913811.2014.947745.

4. Brennan, "Against the Moral Powers Test of Basic Liberty."

5. Patten, "Are the Economic Liberties Basic?"

6. This formulation originates in Rawls and is explained in more detail in von Platz. John Rawls, *Political Liberalism*, Expanded edition (New York: Columbia University Press, 2005), 292–93; Jeppe von Platz, "Are Economic Liberties Basic Rights?" *Politics, Philosophy & Economics* 13, no. 1 (February 1, 2014): 23–44, doi: 10.1177/1470594X13483466.

7. Defenders include Jessica Flanigan, "All Liberty Is Basic." *Res Publica* 24, no. 4 (November 1, 2018): 455–474, doi: 10.1007/s11158-017-9368-z; See also Tomasi, *Free Market Fairness*, 2012; Platz, "Are Economic Liberties Basic Rights?"

8. Flanigan, "All Liberty Is Basic"; Ryan W. Davis, "Self-Authorship and the Claim Against Interference." *Pacific Philosophical Quarterly* 102, no. 2 (2021): 220–242, doi: 10.1111/papq.12336.

9. For discussion, see Brennan, "Against the Moral Powers Test of Basic Liberty."

10. Flanigan, "All Liberty Is Basic"; John Tomasi, *Free Market Fairness*, 2012; Davis, "Self-Authorship and the Claim Against Interference."

11. See, for example, Carlson, *Citizen-Protectors*.

12. Brennan, "Against the Moral Powers Test of Basic Liberty"; Flanigan, "All Liberty Is Basic."

13. Brennan, "Against the Moral Powers Test of Basic Liberty."

14. I'm grateful to a referee for providing me with this case.

15. For a description, see Joe Sutton, "Harvey Updyke, Who Poisoned Iconic Oak Trees at Auburn, Dies at 71," CNN, July 31, 2020, accessed February 14, 2023, https://www.cnn.com/2020/07/31/us/harvey-updyke-alabama-auburn-dead/index.html.

16. Douglas N. Husak, *Overcriminalization: The Limits of the Criminal Law* (Oxford University Press, 2009), 93–95.

17. Stephen Darwall, *The Second-Person Standpoint: Morality, Respect, and Accountability* (Cambridge, MA: Harvard University Press, 2006).

18. Husak, *Overcriminalization*, 98.

19. cf. Christopher Heath Wellman, *Rights Forfeiture and Punishment* (Oxford: Oxford University Press, 2017).

20. Thomas Metcalf, "GUN VIOLENCE AS INDUSTRIAL POLLUTION," n.d., 41.

21. For a sophisticated treatment, see R. A. Duff, *The Realm of Criminal Law* (Oxford: Oxford University Press, 2018).

22. Husak, *Overcriminalization*, 101–102.

5

1. C'Zar Bernstein, Timothy Hsiao, and Matt Palumbo, "THE MORAL RIGHT TO KEEP AND BEAR FIREARMS." *Public Affairs Quarterly* 29, no. 4 (2015): 345–363; John R. Lott, Jr., *More Guns, Less Crime: Understanding Crime and Gun Control Laws* (Chicago, IL: University of Chicago Press, 1998).

2. Cf. LaFollette, *In Defense of Gun Control*.

3. RAND Corporation, "What Science Tells Us About the Effects of Gun Policies." January 10, 2023, https://www.rand.org/research/gun-pol icy/key-findings/what-science-tells-us-about-the-effects-of-gun-poli cies.html.

4. Michael Siegel et al., "The Relation between State Gun Laws and the Incidence and Severity of Mass Public Shootings in the United States, 1976–2018." *Law and Human Behavior* 44, no. 5 (October 2020): 347–360, doi: 10.1037/lhb0000378.

5. Sherry Towers, Danielle Wallace, and David Hemenway, "Temporal Trends in Public Mass Shootings: High-Capacity Magazines Significantly Increase Fatality Counts, and Are Becoming More Prevalent." preprint (Public and Global Health, December 15, 2019), doi: 10.1101/2019. 12.12.19014738.

6. Victoria M. Smith et al., "Broadening the Perspective on Gun Violence: An Examination of the Firearms Industry, 1990–2015." *American Journal of Preventive Medicine* 53, no. 5 (November 2017): 584–591, doi: 10.1016/j.amepre.2017.05.002.

7. Christopher S. Koper et al., "Criminal Use of Assault Weapons and High-Capacity Semiautomatic Firearms: An Updated Examination of Local and National Sources." *Journal of Urban Health* 95, no. 3 (June 1, 2018): 313–321, doi: 10.1007/s11524-017-0205-7.

8. James Alan Fox and Monica J. DeLateur, "Weapons of Mass (Murder) Destruction." *New England Journal on Criminal and Civil Confinement* 40 (2014): 324–325.

9. James B. Jacobs, "Why Ban Assault Weapons." *Cardozo Law Review* 37 (2016 2015): 689.

10. Mark Gius, "The Impact of State and Federal Assault Weapons Bans on Public Mass Shootings." *Applied Economics Letters* 22, no. 4 (March 4, 2015): 281–284, doi: 10.1080/13504851.2014.939367.

11. Gius, 383–384.

12. Siegel et al., "The Relation between State Gun Laws and the Incidence and Severity of Mass Public Shootings in the United States, 1976–2018."; Daniel W. Webster et al., "Evidence Concerning the Regulation of Firearms Design, Sale, and Carrying on Fatal Mass Shootings in the United States." *Criminology & Public Policy* 19, no. 1 (February 2020): 171–212, doi: 10.1111/1745–9133.12487.

13. Ping-I. Lin et al., "What Have We Learned from the Time Trend of Mass Shootings in the U.S.?" *PLOS ONE* 13, no. 10 (October 18, 2018): e0204722, doi: 10.1371/journal.pone.0204722.

14. Siegel et al., "The Relation between State Gun Laws and the Incidence and Severity of Mass Public Shootings in the United States, 1976–2018," 355.

Notes

15. Webster et al., "Evidence Concerning the Regulation of Firearms Design, Sale, and Carrying on Fatal Mass Shootings in the United States," 188.

16. Louis Klarevas, Andrew Conner, and David Hemenway, "The Effect of Large-Capacity Magazine Bans on High-Fatality Mass Shootings, 1990–2017." *American Journal of Public Health* 109, no. 12 (December 2019): 1754–1761, doi: 10.2105/AJPH.2019.305311; Koper et al., "Criminal Use of Assault Weapons and High-Capacity Semiautomatic Firearms."

17. Klarevas, Conner, and Hemenway, "The Effect of Large-Capacity Magazine Bans on High-Fatality Mass Shootings, 1990–2017."

18. Gary Kleck, "Large Capacity Magazines and the Casualty Counts in Mass Shootings: The Plausibility of Linkages/" *Justice Research and Policy* 17:1 (2016).

19. Klarevas, Conner, and Hemenway, "The Effect of Large-Capacity Magazine Bans on High-Fatality Mass Shootings, 1990–2017," 1757.

20. Koper et al., "Criminal Use of Assault Weapons and High-Capacity Semiautomatic Firearms."

21. Simon Chapman et al., "Fatal Firearm Incidents Before and After Australia's 1996 National Firearms Agreement Banning Semiautomatic Rifles." *Annals of Internal Medicine* 169, no. 1 (July 3, 2018): 62–64, doi: 10.7326/M18–0503; Simon Chapman, Philip Alpers, and Michael Jones, "Association Between Gun Law Reforms and Intentional Firearm Deaths in Australia, 1979–2013." *JAMA* 316, no. 3 (July 19, 2016): 291, doi: 10.1001/jama.2016.8752.

22. Andrew Leigh and Christine Neill, "Do Gun Buybacks Save Lives? Evidence from Panel Data." *American Law and Economics Review* 12, no. 2 (October 1, 2010): 509–557, doi: 10.1093/aler/ahq013.

23. Zack Beauchamp, "Australia Confiscated 650,000 Guns. Murders and Suicides Plummeted." Vox, August 27, 2015, https://www.vox.com/2015/8/27/9212725/australia-buyback.

24. Benjamin Taylor and Jing Li, "Do Fewer Guns Lead to Less Crime? Evidence from Australia." *International Review of Law and Economics* 42 (June 2015): 72–78, doi: 10.1016/j.irle.2015.01.002.

25. Stuart Gilmour, Kittima Wattanakamolkul, and Maaya Kita Sugai, "The Effect of the Australian National Firearms Agreement on Suicide and Homicide Mortality, 1978–2015." *American Journal of Public Health* 108, no. 11 (November 2018): 1511–1516, doi: 10.2105/AJPH.2018.304640.

26. Gilmour, Wattanakamolkul, and Sugai, 1515.

27. Michael Siegel, "Implications of the Australian Experience With Firearm Regulation for US Gun Policy." *American Journal of Public Health* 108, no. 11 (November 2018): 1438, doi: 10.2105/AJPH.2018.304720.

28. John R. Lott, Jr. and David B. Mustard, "Crime, Deterrence, and Right-to-Carry Concealed Handguns." *The Journal of Legal Studies* 26, no. 1 (January 1997): 1–68, doi: 10.1086/467988.

29. John J. Donohue, Abhay Aneja, and Kyle D. Weber, "Right-to-Carry Laws and Violent Crime: A Comprehensive Assessment Using Panel Data and a State-Level Synthetic Control Analysis." Working Paper, Working Paper Series (National Bureau of Economic Research, June 2017), doi: 10.3386/w23510.

30. Michael Siegel et al., "Easiness of Legal Access to Concealed Firearm Permits and Homicide Rates in the United States." *American Journal of Public Health* 107, no. 12 (December 2017): 1923–1929, doi: 10.2105/AJPH.2017.304057.

31. Siegel et al., "Easiness of Legal Access to Concealed Firearm Permits and Homicide Rates in the United States."

32. Srikant Devaraj and Pankaj C. Patel, "An Examination of the Effects of 2014 Concealed Weapons Law in Illinois on Property Crimes in Chicago." *Applied Economics Letters* 25, no. 16 (2018): 1125–1129.

33. Mark Gius, "An Examination of the Effects of Concealed Weapons Laws and Assault Weapons Bans on State-Level Murder Rates." *Applied Economics Letters* 21, no. 4 (March 4, 2014): 265–267, doi: 10.1080/13504851.2013.854294.

34. Mehdi Barati, "New Evidence on the Impact of Concealed Carry Weapon Laws on Crime." *International Review of Law and Economics* 47 (August 2016): 76–83, doi: 10.1016/j.irle.2016.05.011; Michael R. Smith and Matthew Petrocelli, "The Effect of Concealed Handgun Carry Deregulation in Arizona on Crime in Tucson." *Criminal Justice Policy Review* 30, no. 8 (October 2019): 1186–1203, doi: 10.1177/0887403418782739.

35. Barati, "New Evidence on the Impact of Concealed Carry Weapon Laws on Crime."

36. David Fortunato, "Can Easing Concealed Carry Deter Crime?" *Social Science Quarterly* 96, no. 4 (December 2015): 1071–1085, doi: 10.1111/ssqu.12166.

37. Kleck and DeLone, "Victim Resistance and Offender Weapon Effects in Robbery." Journal of Quantitative Criminology 9 (1993): 55–81;

Lindegaard, Beransco, and Jacques, "Consequences of Expected and Observed Victim Resistance for Offender Violence during Robbery Events." Journal of Research in Crime & Delinquency 52 (2014): 32–61.

38. Alessandro Acquisti and Catherine Tucker, "Guns, Privacy, and Crime." Working Paper, Working Paper Series (National Bureau of Economic Research, April 2022), doi: 10.3386/w29940.

39. Joseph De Angelis, Terressa A. Benz, and Patrick Gillham, "Collective Security, Fear of Crime, and Support for Concealed Firearms on a University Campus in the Western United States." Criminal Justice Review 42, no. 1 (March 2017): 77–94, doi: 10.1177/0734016816686660.

40. Jill K. Hayter et al., "1 Right-to-Carry and Campus Crime: Evidence from the Not-so-Wild-West," n.d.; Mark Gius, "Campus Crime and Concealed Carry Laws: Is Arming Students the Answer?" The Social Science Journal 56, no. 1 (March 1, 2019): 3–9, doi: 10.1016/j. soscij.2018.04.004.

41. David Card and Gordon B. Dahl, "Family Violence and Football: The Effect of Unexpected Emotional Cues on Violent Behavior." The Quarterly Journal of Economics 126, no. 1 (February 2011): 103–143, doi: 10.1093/qje/qjr001.

42. Christoph Koenig and David Schindler, "Impulse Purchases, Gun Ownership and Homicides: Evidence from a Firearm Demand Shock." SSRN Electronic Journal, 2018, doi: 10.2139/ssrn.3272156.

43. Michael Luca, Deepak Malhotra, and Christopher Poliquin, "Handgun Waiting Periods Reduce Gun Deaths." Proceedings of the National Academy of Sciences 114, no. 46 (November 14, 2017): 12162–12165, doi: 10.1073/pnas.1619896114.

44. Jens Ludwig, "Reducing Gun Violence in America." Proceedings of the National Academy of Sciences 114, no. 46 (November 14, 2017): 12097–12099, doi: 10.1073/pnas.1717306114.

45. Kara E. Rudolph et al., "Association Between Connecticut's Permit-to-Purchase Handgun Law and Homicides." American Journal of Public Health 105, no. 8 (August 2015): e49–54, doi: 10.2105/AJPH.2015.302703.

46. Alvaro Castillo-Carniglia et al., "California's Comprehensive Background Check and Misdemeanor Violence Prohibition Policies and Firearm Mortality." Annals of Epidemiology 30 (February 2019): 50–56, doi: 10.1016/j.annepidem.2018.10.001.

47. Gius, "The Impact of State and Federal Assault Weapons Bans on Public Mass Shootings."

48. For a survey of challenges see Garen J. Wintemute, "Background Checks For Firearm Purchases: Problem Areas And Recommendations To Improve Effectiveness." *Health Affairs* 38, no. 10 (October 1, 2019): 1702–1710, doi: 10.1377/hlthaff.2019.00671.

6

1. For a few general findings about the consequences of gun owner- ship, see Sripal Bangalore and Franz H. Messerli, "Gun Ownership and Firearm-Related Deaths." *The American Journal of Medicine* 126, no. 10 (October 2013): 873–876, doi: 10.1016/j.amjmed.2013.04.012; Charles C. Branas et al., "Investigating the Link Between Gun Possession and Gun Assault." *American Journal of Public Health* 99, no. 11 (November 2009): 2034–2040, doi: 10.2105/AJPH.2008.143099; Michael C. Monuteaux et al., "Firearm Ownership and Violent Crime in the U.S." *American Journal of Preventive Medicine* 49, no. 2 (August 2015): 207–214, doi: 10.1016/j.amepre.2015.02.008; Julian Santaella- Tenorio et al., "What Do We Know About the Association Between Firearm Legislation and Firearm-Related Injuries?" *Epidemiologic Reviews* 38, no. 1 (January 1, 2016): 140–157, doi: 10.1093/epirev/mxv012.

2. PolitiFact, "Does Joe Biden's Plan Tax Semi-Automatic Firearms?," accessed September 27, 2022, https://www.politifact.com/article/2020/nov/01/does-joe-bidens-plan-tax-semi-automatic-firearms/.

3. Kim Kerry, "Biden's Gun Control Plan Is Terrible for Working Class Firearm Owners - The Washington Post," accessed September 27, 2022, https://www.washingtonpost.com/outlook/2020/07/16/biden-gun-control-poverty/.

4. Heather Sher, "What I Saw Treating the Victims From Parkland Should Change the Debate on Guns," *The Atlantic*, February 22, 2018, https://www.theatlantic.com/politics/archive/2018/02/what-i-saw-treating-the-victims-from-parkland-should-change-the-debate-on-guns/553937/.

5. Jon Schuppe, "America's Rifle: Why so Many People Love the AR-15," accessed September 27, 2022, https://www.nbcnews.com/news/us-news/america-s-rifle-why-so-many-people-love-ar-15-n831171.

6. Sergio Pecanha, "Opinion | Lockdown Drills: An American Quirk, out of Control," *Washington Post*, accessed September 27, 2022, https://www.washingtonpost.com/opinions/2019/10/11/lockdown-drills-an-american-quirk-out-control/.

7. John Gramlich, "What the Data Says (and Doesn't Say) about Crime in the United States," *Pew Research Center* (blog), accessed September 27, 2022, https://www.pewresearch.org/fact-tank/2020/11/20/facts-about-crime-in-the-u-s/.

8. "Historical Car Crash Deaths and Rates – Injury Facts," accessed September 27, 2022, https://injuryfacts.nsc.org/motor-vehicle/historical-fatality-trends/deaths-and-rates/.

9. Donald W. Bruckner, "Gun Control and Alcohol Policy." *Social Theory and Practice* 44, no. 2 (2018): 149–177, doi: 10.5840/soctheorpract20185834.

10. Terry L. Schell et al., "Changes in Firearm Mortality Following the Implementation of State Laws Regulating Firearm Access and Use." *Proceedings of the National Academy of Sciences* 117, no. 26 (June 30, 2020): 14906–14910, doi: 10.1073/pnas.1921965117.

11. Centers for Disease Control and Prevention, "Alcohol-Related Deaths," November 15, 2022, https://www.cdc.gov/alcohol/features/excessive-alcohol-deaths.html.

12. Centers for Disease Control and Prevention, "Impaired Driving: Get the Facts | Transportation Safety | Injury Center," December 28, 2022, https://www.cdc.gov/transportationsafety/impaired_driving/impaired-drv_factsheet.html.

13. T. Nagata et al., "Effectiveness of a Law to Reduce Alcohol-Impaired Driving in Japan." *Injury Prevention* 14, no. 1 (February 1, 2008): 19–23, doi: 10.1136/ip.2007.015719.

14. Peter Lyon, "This Is What Zero Tolerance For Drink Driving Looks Like," *Forbes*, accessed March 6, 2023, https://www.forbes.com/sites/peterlyon/2020/08/27/frightening-consequences-for-drink-drivers-in-japan/.

15. "Texting and Driving Accident Statistics – Distracted Driving," edgarsnyder.com, accessed September 27, 2022, https://www.edgarsnyder.com/car-accident/cause-of-accident/cell-phone/cell-phone-statistics.html.

16. Gramlich, "What the Data Says (and Doesn't Say) about Crime in the United States."

17. Centers for Disease Control and Prevention, "CDC VitalSigns – Preventable Deaths from Heart Disease & Stroke," September 3, 2013, https://www.cdc.gov/vitalsigns/heartdisease-stroke/index.html.

18. Schuppe, "America's Rifle: Why so Many People Love the AR-15."

19. Daniel S. Nagin, Christopher S. Koper, and Cynthia Lum, "Policy Recommendations for Countering Mass Shootings in the United States." *Criminology & Public Policy* 19, no. 1 (February 2020): 9–15, doi: 10.1111/1745-9133.12484.

20. Carolina Díez et al., "State Intimate Partner Violence–Related Firearm Laws and Intimate Partner Homicide Rates in the United States, 1991 to 2015." *Annals of Internal Medicine* 167, no. 8 (October 17, 2017): 536, doi: 10.7326/M16-2849.

21. Frederick Vars and Ian Ayres, "Suicide Accounts for Most Gun Deaths. A Libertarian Approach Could Help. – WSJ," accessed September 27, 2022,https://www.wsj.com/articles/suicide-accounts-for-most-gun-deaths-a-libertarian-approach-could-help-11602717798; Fredrick E. Vars and Angela Selvaggio, "'Bind Me More Tightly Still': Voluntary Restraint Against Gun Suicide." SSRN Scholarly Paper (Rochester, NY, August 7, 2015), doi: 10.2139/ssrn.2641139.

22. Laqueur and Wintemute, "Identifying High Risk Firearm Owners to Prevent Mass Violence." *Criminology & Public Policy* 19:1 (2020): 109–127; Nagin, Koper and Lum, ibid.

23. Nagin, Koper, and Lum, "Policy Recommendations for Countering Mass Shootings in the United States"; Joshua D. Freilich, Steven M. Chermak, and Brent R. Klein, "Investigating the Applicability of Situational Crime Prevention to the Public Mass Violence Context." *Criminology & Public Policy* 19, no. 1 (2020): 271–293, doi: 10.1111/1745-9133.12480.

24. Vars and Ayres, "Suicide Accounts for Most Gun Deaths. A Libertarian Approach Could Help. – WSJ."

25. Cass R. Sunstein, "Sludge Audits." *Behavioural Public Policy*, January 6, 2020, 1–20, doi: 10.1017/bpp.2019.32.

26. RAND Corporation, "What Science Tells Us About the Effects of Gun Policies."

7

1. Philip Pettit, *Republicanism: A Theory of Freedom and Government*, 1st edition (Oxford and New York: Clarendon Press, 1997); Christian List and

Laura Valentini, "Freedom as Independence." *Ethics* 126, no. 4 (July 2016): 1043–1074, doi: 10.1086/686006.

2. Andreas T. Schmidt, "Domination without Inequality? Mutual Domination, Republicanism, and Gun Control." *Philosophy & Public Affairs* 46, no. 2 (April 2018): 175–206, doi: 10.1111/papa.12119.

3. Nelson Lund, "The Future of the Second Amendment in a Time of Lawless Violence." SSRN Scholarly Paper (Rochester, NY, September 28, 2020), doi: 10.2139/ssrn.3701185.

4. Philip Pettit, *On the People's Terms: A Republican Theory and Model of Democracy*, The Seeley Lectures (Cambridge: Cambridge University Press, 2012), doi: 10.1017/CBO9781139017428; An important recent discussion is Dorothea Gädeke, "Does a Mugger Dominate? Episodic Power and the Structural Dimension of Domination." *Journal of Political Philosophy* 28, no. 2 (June 2020): 199–221, doi: 10.1111/jopp.12202.

5. Pettit, *Republicanism*, 52; Gädeke, "Does a Mugger Dominate?," 200.

6. Pettit, *Republicanism*, 87.

7. Pettit, *On the People's Terms*, 47; Frank Lovett and Philip Pettit, "Preserving Republican Freedom: A Reply to Simpson." *Philosophy & Public Affairs* 46, no. 4 (2018): 366, doi: 10.1111/papa.12126.

8. Lovett and Pettit, "Preserving Republican Freedom," 364.

9. Pettit 2012, pp. 2, 63.

10. Pettit, *Republicanism*, 69.

11. Pettit, 54.

12. Frank Lovett, "What Counts as Arbitrary Power?" *Journal of Political Power* 5, no.1 (April 1, 2012): 137–152, doi: 10.1080/2158379X.2012.660026.

13. Schmidt, "Domination without Inequality?," 180.

14. Schmidt, 200.

15. Schmidt, 204 Here I've focused on Schmidt's distinctively republican account, but the idea that possession of firearms itself contributes to morally significant disvalue is more common.

16. Keith Dowding, "Republican Freedom, Rights, and the Coalition Problem." *Politics, Philosophy & Economics* 10, no. 3 (August 1, 2011): 204, doi: 10.1177/1470594X10388380. The problem with expanding the concept is that if too many potential groups count as dominating, then the ubiquity of such groups will mean that domination is always present. This would render republican freedom impossible. This objection is formulated in Dowding, "Republican Freedom, Rights, and the Coalition Problem."

17. Gädeke, "Does a Mugger Dominate?," 205–209. I follow her account here.

18. An affirmative answer is given in Thomas W. Simpson, "The Impossibility of Republican Freedom." *Philosophy & Public Affairs* 45, no. 1 (2017): 27–53, doi: 10.1111/papa.12082; For debate, see Lovett and Pettit, "Preserving Republican Freedom."

19. Lovett and Pettit, "Preserving Republican Freedom," 367–377; For a related solution emphasizing feasibility, see Hallvard Sandven, "Systemic Domination, Social Institutions and the Coalition Problem." *Politics, Philosophy & Economics* 19, no. 4 (November 2020): 382–402, doi: 10.1177/1470594X20927927.

20. Lovett and Pettit, "Preserving Republican Freedom," 378.

21. See, for discussion, Carlson, *Citizen-Protectors*; Lacey N. Wallace, "Concealed Ownership: Americans' Perceived Comfort Sharing Gun Ownership Status with Others." *Sociological Spectrum* 37, no. 5 (September 3, 2017): 267–81, doi: 10.1080/02732173.2017.1348278; Bindu Kalesan et al., "Gun Ownership and Social Gun Culture." *Injury Prevention: Journal of the International Society for Child and Adolescent Injury Prevention* 22, no. 3 (June 2016): 216–220, doi: 10.1136/injuryprev-2015–041586.

22. Schmidt, "Domination without Inequality?," 204.

23. Schmidt, 201–202.

8

1. Alexander Hamilton, John Jay, and James Madison, *The Federalist Papers* (Newburyport, UNITED STATES: Open Road Integrated Media, Inc., 2017), number 46, http://ebookcentral.proquest.com/lib/byu/detail.action?docID=6120004.

2. David Kopel, "Why the Anti-Tyranny Case for the 2nd Amendment Shouldn't Be Dismissed so Quickly," Vox, August 22, 2016, https://www.vox.com/2016/8/22/12559364/second-amendment-tyranny-militia-constitution-founders; David Williams, "Civic Republicanism and the Citizen Militia: The Terrifying Second Amendment." *Yale Law Journal*, January 1, 1991, https://openyls.law.yale.edu/handle/20.500.13051/8675.

3. An important recent exception is Dustin Crummett, "Freedom, Firearms, and Civil Resistance." *The Journal of Ethics* 25, no. 2 (June 1, 2021): 247–266, doi: 10.1007/s10892-021-09365-3 This chapter

was written independently of Crummett's paper, but takes a similar line, with the exception of favoring a personal right to gun ownership.

4. Garrett Epps, "Constitutional Myth #6: The Second Amendment Allows Citizens to Threaten Government," *The Atlantic*, June 30, 2011, https://www.theatlantic.com/national/archive/2011/06/constitutional-myth-6-the-second-amendment-allows-citizens-to-threaten-govern ment/241298/; Michael Shermer, "Opinion | Guns Aren't a Bulwark Against Tyranny. The Rule of Law Is," *The New York Times*, October 5, 2017, sec. Opinion, https://www.nytimes.com/2017/10/05/opinion/gun-rights-vegas-massacre.html.

5. McMahan, "Why Gun 'Control' Is Not Enough."

6. Firmin DeBrabander, *Do Guns Make Us Free?: Democracy and the Armed Society* (New Haven, CT and London: Yale University Press, 2015), 89.

7. DeGrazia and Hunt, *Debating Gun Control*, 190; See Crummett for a helpful discussion of the foregoing passages. Crummett, "Freedom, Firearms, and Civil Resistance," 251–252.

8. DeBrabander, *Do Guns Make Us Free?*, 104.

9. cf. Sanford Levinson, "The Embarrassing Second Amendment." *The Yale Law Journal* 99, no. 3 (1989): 647, doi: 10.2307/796759. Thanks to a referee for encouraging discussion of these issues.

10. Ctd. in Levinson, 649.

11. For a fair minded discussion of the historical meaning of the second amendment, see Joseph Blocher and Darrell A. H. Miller, *The Positive Second Amendment: Rights, Regulation, and the Future of Heller* (Cambridge, UK and New York: Cambridge University Press, 2018), chap. 2.

12. Pettit, *On the People's Terms*, 133; Sandven recounts that "non-domi-nation" is definitionally tied to the rule of law." Sandven, "Systemic Domination, Social Institutions and the Coalition Problem," 3.

13. Pettit, *Republicanism*, 67–68.

14. Pettit, 68.

15. Pettit, 68.

16. Ashley Remkus, "We Spent A Year Investigating Police Dogs. Here Are Six Takeaways," The Marshall Project, October 2, 2020, https://www.themarshallproject.org/2020/10/02/we-spent-a-year-investi gating-police-dogs-here-are-six-takeaways.

17. Jonathan Levinson et al., "Federal Officers Use Unmarked Vehicles To Grab People In Portland, DHS Confirms," *NPR*, July 17, 2020,

sec. America Reckons With Racial Injustice, https://www.npr.org/ 2020/07/17/892277592/federal-officers-use-unmarked-vehicles-to-grab-protesters-in-portland; David Welna, "Democrats Call For Anonymous Policing Of Protests To End," NPR, June 4, 2020, https:// www.npr.org/2020/06/04/870048760/no-names-no-insignias-democrats-call-for-anonymous-policing-of-protests-to-end.

18. Rachel Brown and Coleman Saunders, "Can Law Enforcement Officers Refuse to Identify Themselves?," Lawfare, June 12, 2020, https:// www.lawfareblog.com/can-law-enforcement-officers-refuse-identify-themselves.

19. Joe Soss and Vesla Weaver, "Police Are Our Government: Politics, Political Science, and the Policing of Race–Class Subjugated Communities." Annual Review of Political Science 20, no. 1 (2017): 565–591, doi: 10.1146/annurev-polisci-060415-093825.

20. Soss and Weaver, 572; Sarah Brayne, "Big Data Surveillance: The Case of Policing." American Sociological Review 82, no. 5 (2017), accessed October 1, 2022, doi: 10.1177/0003122417725865.

21. Vesla M. Weaver and Gwen Prowse, "Racial Authoritarianism in U.S. Democracy." Science 369, no. 6508 (September 4, 2020): 1176–78, doi: 10.1126/science.abd7669.

22. Vesla Weaver, Gwen Prowse, and Spencer Piston, "Too Much Knowledge, Too Little Power: An Assessment of Political Knowledge in Highly Policed Communities." The Journal of Politics 81, no. 3 (July 2019): 1164, doi: 10.1086/703538.

23. Joanna Schwartz, "The Case Against Qualified Immunity." Notre Dame Law Review 93, no. 5 (August 1, 2018): 1797.

24. Cathy J. Cohen, Democracy Remixed: Black Youth and the Future of American Politics, 1st edition (Oxford and New York: Oxford University Press, 2010), 141.

25. Cohen notes this interpretation without endorsement. Cohen, 141; Guy Aitchison, "Domination and Disobedience: Protest, Coercion and the Limits of an Appeal to Justice." Perspectives on Politics 16, no. 3 (September 2018): 666–679, doi: 10.1017/S1537592718001111.

26. Tay Wiles, "How the Feds Helped Make Cliven Bundy a Celebrity," High Country News, April 30, 2018, https://www.hcn.org/issues/50.7/sagebrush-rebellion-celebrity-scofflaw; there are several book length treatments. Anthony McCann, Shadowlands: Fear and Freedom at the Oregon

Standoff, 1st Edition (New York: Bloomsbury Publishing, 2019); James Pogue, *Chosen Country: A Rebellion in the West* (New York: Henry Holt and Co., 2018); Christopher Ketcham, *This Land: How Cowboys, Capitalism, and Corruption Are Ruining the American West*, 1st Edition (New York: Viking, 2019).

27. Pema Levy, "A Federal Judge Just Threw out the Case against Cliven Bundy," *Mother Jones* (blog), accessed October 1, 2022, https://www.motherjones.com/politics/2018/01/a-federal-judge-just-threw-out-the-case-against-cliven-bundy/.

28. Associated Press, "Bundy Case: Judge Declares Mistrial Over 2014 Armed Standoff," 20 December 2017. https://www.nbcnews.com/news/us-news/bundy-standoff-judge-declares-mistrial-case-over-2014-armed-standoff-n831526 Accessed 10 October 2020.

29. "United States v. Bundy, 968 F.3d 1019 | Casetext Search + Citator," accessed October 10, 2022, https://casetext.com/case/united-states-v-bundy-95.

30. For a philosophical defense of the use of force in the civil rights movement, see Jill Gordon, "By Any Means Necessary: John Locke and Malcolm X on the Right to Revolution." *Journal of Social Philosophy* 26, no. 1 (1995): 53–85, doi: 10.1111/j.1467–9833.1995.tb00057.x; Chris Suprenant, "Minority Oppression and Justified Revolution," accessed October 1, 2022, https://onlinelibrary.wiley.com/doi/abs/10.1111/j.1467-9833.2010.01509.x.

31. Simon Wendt, "Protection or Path Toward Revolution?: Black Power and Self-Defense." *Souls* 9, no. 4 (December 6, 2007): 320–332, doi: 10.1080/10999940701703778.

32. Simon Wendt, *The Spirit and the Shotgun: Armed Resistance and the Struggle for Civil Rights*, 1st edition (Gainesville, FL: University Press of Florida, 2007), 134–145. It was during Meredith's "march against fear" that Stokley Carmichael introduced the term "black power" into the civil rights lexicon.

33. Ctd. in Christopher B. Strain, *Pure Fire: Self-Defense as Activism in the Civil Rights Era* (Athens, GA: University of Georgia Press, 2005), 120.

34. For discussion see Meredith Roman, "The Black Panther Party and the Struggle for Human Rights." *Spectrum: A Journal on Black Men* 5, no. 1 (2016): 7–32, doi: 10.2979/spectrum.5.1.02; Bridgette Baldwin, "In the Shadow of the Gun: The Black Panther Party, the Ninth Amendment,

and the Discourses of Self-Defense," in *In Search of the Black Panther Party: New Perspectives on a Revolutionary Movement*, ed. Jama Lazerow and Yohuru Williams (Durham, NC: Duke University Press Books, 2006), 67–96.

35. Emilye Crosby, "It Wasn't the Wild West," in *Civil Rights History from the Ground Up: Local Struggles, a National Movement*, ed. Emilye Crosby, Illustrated edition (Athens, GA: University of Georgia Press, 2011); Joe Street, *The Culture War in the Civil Rights Movement*, 1st edition (Gainesville, FL: University Press of Florida, 2007), 137.

36. Crosby, "It Wasn't the Wild West," 196.

37. Michael D. Makowsky and Patrick L. Warren, "Firearms and Lynching." SSRN Scholarly Paper (Rochester, NY, August 7, 2022), 4, doi: 10.2139/ssrn.3727462.

38. Makowsky and Warren, "Firearms and Lynching."

39. Ctd. in Strain, *Pure Fire*, 121.

40. Simon Wendt, "'They Finally Found Out That We Really Are Men': Violence, Non-Violence and Black Manhood in the Civil Rights Era." *Gender & History* 19, no. 3 (2007): 543–564, doi: 10.1111/j.1468-0424.2007.00487.x.

41. Davis, "Symbolic Values."

42. For a discussion of how guns can help maintain the dignity of those subject to injustice, see Dan Demetriou, "Defense with Dignity: How the Dignity of Violent Resistance Informs the Gun Rights Debate." *Philosophical Studies*, August 4, 2022, doi: 10.1007/s11098-022-01856-9.

43. Schmidt, "Domination without Inequality?," 202.

44. Here I make common cause with Bruckner, "Gun Control and Alcohol Policy."

45. Schmidt, "Domination without Inequality?," 205.

46. Schmidt, 205.

Acquisti, Alessandro, and Catherine Tucker. "Guns, Privacy, and Crime." Working Paper. Working Paper Series. National Bureau of Economic Research, April 2022. doi: 10.3386/w29940.

Aitchison, Guy. "Domination and Disobedience: Protest, Coercion and the Limits of an Appeal to Justice." *Perspectives on Politics* 16, no. 3 (September 2018): 666–679. doi: 10.1017/S1537592718001111.

Arnold, Samuel. "The Difference Principle at Work." *Journal of Political Philosophy* 20, no. 1 (2012): 94–118. doi: 10.1111/j.1467–9760.2010.00393.x.

Baldwin, Bridgette. "In the Shadow of the Gun: The Black Panther Party, the Nineth Amendment, and the Discourses of Self-Defense." In *In Search of the Black Panther Party: New Perspectives on a Revolutionary Movement*, edited by Jama Lazerow and Yohuru Williams, 67–96. Durham, NC: Duke University Press Books, 2006.

Bangalore, Sripal, and Franz H. Messerli. "Gun Ownership and Firearm-Related Deaths." *The American Journal of Medicine* 126, no. 10 (October 2013): 873–876. doi: 10.1016/j.amjmed.2013.04.012.

Barati, Mehdi. "New Evidence on the Impact of Concealed Carry Weapon Laws on Crime." *International Review of Law and Economics* 47 (August 2016): 76–83. doi: 10.1016/j.irle.2016.05.011.

Beauchamp, Zack. "Australia Confiscated 650,000 Guns. Murders and Suicides Plummeted." Vox, August 27, 2015. https://www.vox.com/2015/8/27/9212725/australia-buyback.

Bernstein, C'Zar, Timothy Hsiao, and Matt Palumbo. "THE MORAL RIGHT TO KEEP AND BEAR FIREARMS." *Public Affairs Quarterly* 29, no. 4 (2015): 345–363.

Blanco, Dennis Vicencio. "The Gun Control Debate: Why Experience and Culture Matters." *International Journal of Public Administration* 39, no. 8 (July 2, 2016): 620–634. doi: 10.1080/01900692.2015.1028639.

Blocher, Joseph, and Darrell A. H. Miller. *The Positive Second Amendment: Rights, Regulation, and the Future of Heller*. Cambridge, UK and New York: Cambridge University Press, 2018.

Branas, Charles C., Therese S. Richmond, Dennis P. Culhane, Thomas R. Ten Have, and Douglas J. Wiebe. "Investigating the Link Between Gun Possession and Gun Assault." *American Journal of Public Health* 99, no. 11 (November 2009): 2034–2040. doi: 10.2105/AJPH.2008.143099.

Brayne, Sarah. "Big Data Surveillance: The Case of Policing." *American Sociological Review* 82, no. 5 (2017). Accessed October 1, 2022. https://journals.sagepub.com/doi/10.1177/0003122417725865.

Brennan, Jason. "Against the Moral Powers Test of Basic Liberty." *European Journal of Philosophy* 28, no. 2 (2020): 492–505. doi: 10.1111/ejop.12497.

Bruckner, Donald W. "Gun Control and Alcohol Policy." *Social Theory and Practice* 44, no. 2 (2018): 149–177. doi: 10.5840/soctheorpract20185834.

Brown, Rachel and Saunders, Coleman. "Can Law Enforcement Officers Refuse to Identify Themselves?" *Lawfare*, June 12, 2020. https://www.lawfareblog.com/can-law-enforcement-officers-refuse-identify-themselves.

Card, David, and Gordon B. Dahl. "Family Violence and Football: The Effect of Unexpected Emotional Cues on Violent Behavior." *The Quarterly Journal of Economics* 126, no. 1 (February 2011): 103–143. doi: 10.1093/qje/qjr001.

Carlson, Jennifer. *Citizen-Protectors: The Everyday Politics of Guns in an Age of Decline*. Oxford and New York: Oxford University Press, 2018.

Castillo-Carniglia, Alvaro, Rose M. C. Kagawa, Magdalena Cerdá, Cassandra K. Crifasi, Jon S. Vernick, Daniel W. Webster, and Garen J. Wintemute. "California's Comprehensive Background Check and Misdemeanor Violence Prohibition Policies and Firearm Mortality." *Annals of Epidemiology* 30 (February 2019): 50–56. doi: 10.1016/j.annepidem.2018.10.001.

Centers for Disease Control and Prevention. "Impaired Driving: Get the Facts | Transportation Safety | Injury Center." December 28, 2022. https://www.cdc.gov/transportationsafety/impaired_driving/impaired-drv_factsheet.html.

——. "Alcohol-Related Deaths." November 15, 2022. https://www.cdc.gov/alcohol/features/excessive-alcohol-deaths.html.

——. "CDC VitalSigns – Preventable Deaths from Heart Disease & Stroke." Centers for Disease Control and Prevention, September 3, 2013. https://www.cdc.gov/vitalsigns/heartdisease-stroke/index.html.

Why It's OK to Own a Gun

Celinska, Katarzyna. "Individualism and Collectivism in America: The Case of Gun Ownership and Attitudes toward Gun Control." *Sociological Perspectives* 50, no. 2 (June 2007): 229–247. doi: 10.1525/sop.2007. 50.2.229.

Chapman, Simon, Philip Alpers, and Michael Jones. "Association Between Gun Law Reforms and Intentional Firearm Deaths in Australia, 1979–2013." *JAMA* 316, no. 3 (July 19, 2016): 291. doi: 10.1001/jama.2016.8752.

Chapman, Simon, Michael Stewart, Philip Alpers, and Michael Jones. "Fatal Firearm Incidents Before and After Australia's 1996 National Firearms Agreement Banning Semiautomatic Rifles." *Annals of Internal Medicine* 169, no. 1 (July 3, 2018): 62–64. doi: 10.7326/M18–0503.

Cohen, Cathy J. *Democracy Remixed: Black Youth and the Future of American Politics.* 1st edition. Oxford and New York: Oxford University Press, 2010.

Cohen, G. A. "The Structure of Proletarian Unfreedom." *Philosophy & Public Affairs* 12, no. 1 (1983): 3–33.

Cramer, Katherine J. *The Politics of Resentment: Rural Consciousness in Wisconsin and the Rise of Scott Walker.* Illustrated edition. Chicago, IL and London: University of Chicago Press, 2016.

Crosby, Emilye. "It Wasn't the Wild West." In *Civil Rights History from the Ground Up: Local Struggles, a National Movement*, edited by Emilye Crosby, Illustrated edition. Athens, GA: University of Georgia Press, 2011.

Crummett, Dustin. "Freedom, Firearms, and Civil Resistance." *The Journal of Ethics* 25, no. 2 (June 1, 2021): 247–266. doi: 10.1007/s10892-021-09365-3.

Crummett, Dustin, and Philip Swenson. "Gun Control, the Right to Self-Defense, and Reasonable Beneficence to All." *Ergo, an Open Access Journal of Philosophy* 6, no. 20201214 (October 16, 2019). doi: 10.3998/ergo. 12405314.0006.036.

Darwall, Stephen. *The Second-Person Standpoint: Morality, Respect, and Accountability.* Cambridge, MA: Harvard University Press, 2006.

Davis, Ryan W. "Self-Authorship and the Claim Against Interference." *Pacific Philosophical Quarterly* 102, no. 2 (2021): 220–242. doi: 10.1111/papq. 12336.

——. "Symbolic Values." *Journal of the American Philosophical Association* 5, no. 4 (2019): 449–67. doi: 10.1017/apa.2019.25.

De Angelis, Joseph, Terressa A. Benz, and Patrick Gillham. "Collective Security, Fear of Crime, and Support for Concealed Firearms on a University Campus in the Western United States." *Criminal Justice Review* 42, no. 1 (March 2017): 77–94. doi: 10.1177/0734016816686660.

DeBrabander, Firmin. *Do Guns Make Us Free?: Democracy and the Armed Society*. New Haven, CT and London: Yale University Press, 2015.

DeGrazia, David, and Lester H. Hunt. *Debating Gun Control: How Much Regulation Do We Need?* 1st edition. New York: Oxford University Press, 2016.

Demetriou, Dan. "Defense with Dignity: How the Dignity of Violent Resistance Informs the Gun Rights Debate." *Philosophical Studies*, August 4, 2022. doi: 10.1007/s11098-022-01856-9.

Díez, Carolina, Rachel P. Kurland, Emily F. Rothman, Megan Bair-Merritt, Eric Fleegler, Ziming Xuan, Sandro Galea, et al. "State Intimate Partner Violence–Related Firearm Laws and Intimate Partner Homicide Rates in the United States, 1991 to 2015." *Annals of Internal Medicine* 167, no. 8 (October 17, 2017): 536. doi: 10.7326/M16-2849.

Donohue, John J., Abhay Aneja, and Kyle D. Weber. "Right-to-Carry Laws and Violent Crime: A Comprehensive Assessment Using Panel Data and a State-Level Synthetic Control Analysis." Working Paper. Working Paper Series. National Bureau of Economic Research, June 2017. doi: 10.3386/w23510.

Dowding, Keith. "Republican Freedom, Rights, and the Coalition Problem." *Politics, Philosophy & Economics* 10, no. 3 (August 1, 2011): 301–322. doi: 10.1177/1470594X10388380.

Duff, R. A. *The Realm of Criminal Law*. Oxford: Oxford University Press, 2018.

edgarsnyder.com. "Texting and Driving Accident Statistics – Distracted Driving." Accessed September 27, 2022. https://www.edgarsnyder.com/car-accident/cause-of-accident/cell-phone/cell-phone-statistics.html.

Epps, Garrett. "Constitutional Myth #6: The Second Amendment Allows Citizens to Threaten Government." *The Atlantic*, June 30, 2011. https://www.theatlantic.com/national/archive/2011/06/constitutional-myth-6-the-second-amendment-allows-citizens-to-threaten-government/241298/.

Flanigan, Jessica. "All Liberty Is Basic." *Res Publica* 24, no. 4 (November 1, 2018): 455–474. doi: 10.1007/s11158-017-9368-z.

Fortunato, David. "Can Easing Concealed Carry Deter Crime?: Can Easing Concealed Carry Deter Crime?" *Social Science Quarterly* 96, no. 4 (December 2015): 1071–1085. doi: 10.1111/ssqu.12166.

Fox, James Alan, and Monica J. DeLateur. "Weapons of Mass (Murder) Destruction." *New England Journal on Criminal and Civil Confinement* 40 (2014): 313.

Freeman, Samuel. *Rawls*. Abingdon, UK and New York: Routledge, 2007.

Freilich, Joshua D., Steven M. Chermak, and Brent R. Klein. "Investigating the Applicability of Situational Crime Prevention to the Public Mass Violence Context." *Criminology & Public Policy* 19, no. 1 (2020): 271–293. doi: 10.1111/1745–9133.12480.

Gädeke, Dorothea. "Does a Mugger Dominate? Episodic Power and the Structural Dimension of Domination." *Journal of Political Philosophy* 28, no. 2 (June 2020): 199–221. doi: 10.1111/jopp.12202.

Gilmour, Stuart, Kittima Wattanakamolkul, and Maaya Kita Sugai. "The Effect of the Australian National Firearms Agreement on Suicide and Homicide Mortality, 1978–2015." *American Journal of Public Health* 108, no. 11 (November 2018): 1511–1516. doi: 10.2105/AJPH.2018.304640.

Gius, Mark. "An Examination of the Effects of Concealed Weapons Laws and Assault Weapons Bans on State-Level Murder Rates." *Applied Economics Letters* 21, no. 4 (March 4, 2014): 265–267. doi: 10.1080/13504851.2013.854294.

——. "Campus Crime and Concealed Carry Laws: Is Arming Students the Answer?" *The Social Science Journal* 56, no. 1 (March 1, 2019): 3–9. doi: 10.1016/j.soscij.2018.04.004.

——. "The Impact of State and Federal Assault Weapons Bans on Public Mass Shootings." *Applied Economics Letters* 22, no. 4 (March 4, 2015): 281–284. doi: 10.1080/13504851.2014.939367.

Gordon, Jill. "By Any Means Necessary: John Locke and Malcolm X on the Right to Revolution." *Journal of Social Philosophy* 26, no. 1 (1995): 53–85. doi: 10.1111/j.1467–9833.1995.tb00057.x.

Gramlich, John. "What the Data Says (and Doesn't Say) about Crime in the United States." *Pew Research Center* (blog). Accessed September 27, 2022. https://www.pewresearch.org/fact-tank/2020/11/20/facts-about-crime-in-the-u-s/.

Hamilton, Alexander, John Jay, and James Madison. *The Federalist Papers*. Newburyport, UNITED STATES: Open Road Integrated Media, Inc., 2017. http://ebookcentral.proquest.com/lib/byu/detail.action?docID=6120004.

Hare, Caspar. "Should We Wish Well to All?" *The Philosophical Review* 125, no. 4 (October 1, 2016): 451–472. doi: 10.1215/00318108–3624764.

Hayter, Jill K., Gary L. Shelley, Taylor, and P. Stevenson. "1 Right-to-Carry and Campus Crime: Evidence from the Not-so-Wild-West," n.d.

"Historical Car Crash Deaths and Rates – Injury Facts." Accessed September 27, 2022. https://injuryfacts.nsc.org/motor-vehicle/historical-fatality-trends/deaths-and-rates/.

Huemer, Michael. "Gun Rights as Deontic Constraints." *Social Theory and Practice* 45, no. 4 (November 1, 2019): 601–612. doi: 10.5840/soctheorpract20201375.

———. "Is There a Right to Own a Gun?" *Social Theory and Practice* 29, no. 2 (May 1, 2003): 297–324. doi: 10.5840/soctheorpract200329215.

Husak, Douglas N. *Overcriminalization: The Limits of the Criminal Law.* Oxford: Oxford University Press, 2009.

Jacobs, James B. "Why Ban Assault Weapons." *Cardozo Law Review* 37 (2016 2015): 681.

Kalesan, Bindu, Marcos D Villarreal, Katherine M Keyes, and Sandro Galea. "Gun Ownership and Social Gun Culture." *Injury Prevention* 22, no. 3 (June 2016): 216–220. doi: 10.1136/injuryprev-2015–041586.

Kalesan, Bindu, Marcos D. Villarreal, Katherine M. Keyes, and Sandro Galea. "Gun Ownership and Social Gun Culture." *Injury Prevention: Journal of the International Society for Child and Adolescent Injury Prevention* 22, no. 3 (June 2016): 216–220. doi: 10.1136/injuryprev-2015–041586.

Kamm, F. M. *Intricate Ethics: Rights, Responsibilities, and Permissible Harm.* Oxford: Oxford University Press, 2008.

Kant, Immanuel. *Critique Of Judgement, The.* South Bend, UNITED STATES: Infomotions, Inc., 2000. http://ebookcentral.proquest.com/lib/byu/detail.action?docID=3314533.

Kerry, Kim. "Biden's Gun Control Plan Is Terrible for Working Class Firearm Owners - The Washington Post." Accessed September 27, 2022. https://www.washingtonpost.com/outlook/2020/07/16/biden-gun-control-poverty/.

Ketcham, Christopher. *This Land: How Cowboys, Capitalism, and Corruption Are Ruining the American West.* 1st Edition. New York: Viking, 2019.

Klarevas, Louis, Andrew Conner, and David Hemenway. "The Effect of Large-Capacity Magazine Bans on High-Fatality Mass Shootings, 1990–2017." *American Journal of Public Health* 109, no. 12 (December 2019): 1754–1761. doi: 10.2105/AJPH.2019.305311.

Kleef, Gerben A van, and Jens Lange. "How Hierarchy Shapes Our Emotional Lives: Effects of Power and Status on Emotional Experience, Expression, and Responsiveness." *Current Opinion in Psychology*, Power, Status and Hierarchy, 33 (June 1, 2020): 148–153. doi: 10.1016/j.copsyc.2019.07.009.

Koenig, Christoph, and David Schindler. "Impulse Purchases, Gun Ownership and Homicides: Evidence from a Firearm Demand Shock." *SSRN Electronic Journal*, 2018. doi: 10.2139/ssrn.3272156.

Kopel, David. "Why the Anti-Tyranny Case for the 2nd Amendment Shouldn't Be Dismissed so Quickly." Vox, August 22, 2016. https://www.vox.com/2016/8/22/12559364/second-amendment-tyranny-militia-constitution-founders.

Koper, Christopher S., William D. Johnson, Jordan L. Nichols, Ambrozine Ayers, and Natalie Mullins. "Criminal Use of Assault Weapons and High-Capacity Semiautomatic Firearms: An Updated Examination of Local and National Sources." *Journal of Urban Health* 95, no. 3 (June 1, 2018): 313–321. doi: 10.1007/s11524-017-0205-7.

Korsgaard, Christine M. *Creating the Kingdom of Ends*. Cambridge: Cambridge University Press, 1996. doi: 10.1017/CBO9781139174503.

——. "Two Distinctions in Goodness." *The Philosophical Review* 92, no. 2 (1983): 169–195. doi: 10.2307/2184924.

Kruis, Nathan E., Richard L. Wentling, Tyler S. Frye, and Nicholas J. Rowland. "Firearm Ownership, Defensive Gun Usage, and Support for Gun Control: Does Knowledge Matter?" *American Journal of Criminal Justice*, September 30, 2021. doi: 10.1007/s12103-021-09644-7.

LaFollette, Hugh. *In Defense of Gun Control*. New York: Oxford University Press, 2018.

Lear, Jonathan. *Radical Hope: Ethics in the Face of Cultural Devastation*. Cambridge, MA and London: Harvard University Press, 2008.

Leigh, Andrew, and Christine Neill. "Do Gun Buybacks Save Lives? Evidence from Panel Data." *American Law and Economics Review* 12, no. 2 (October 1, 2010): 509–557. doi: 10.1093/aler/ahq013.

Levinson, Jonathan, Conrad Wilson, James Doubek, and Suzanne Nuyen. "Federal Officers Use Unmarked Vehicles To Grab People In Portland, DHS Confirms." NPR, July 17, 2020, sec. America Reckons With Racial Injustice. https://www.npr.org/2020/07/17/892277592/federal-officers-use-unmarked-vehicles-to-grab-protesters-in-portland.

Levinson, Sanford. "The Embarrassing Second Amendment." *The Yale Law Journal* 99, no. 3 (1989): 637–659. doi: 10.2307/796759.

Levy, Pema. "A Federal Judge Just Threw out the Case against Cliven Bundy." *Mother Jones* (blog). Accessed October 1, 2022. https://www.motherjones.com/politics/2018/01/a-federal-judge-just-threw-out-the-case-against-cliven-bundy/.

Lin, Ping-I., Lin Fei, Drew Barzman, and M. Hossain. "What Have We Learned from the Time Trend of Mass Shootings in the U.S.?" *PLOS ONE* 13, no. 10 (October 18, 2018): e0204722. doi: 10.1371/journal.pone.0204722.

List, Christian, and Laura Valentini. "Freedom as Independence." *Ethics* 126, no. 4 (July 2016): 1043–1074. doi: 10.1086/686006.

Locke, John. *Locke : Two Treatises of Government*. Cambridge, UK and New York: Cambridge University Press, 1988.

Lott, Jr., John R. *More Guns, Less Crime: Understanding Crime and Gun Control Laws*. Chicago, IL: University of Chicago Press, 1998.

Lott, Jr., John R., and David B. Mustard. "Crime, Deterrence, and Right-to-Carry Concealed Handguns." *The Journal of Legal Studies* 26, no. 1 (January 1997): 1–68. doi: 10.1086/467988.

Lovett, Frank. "What Counts as Arbitrary Power?" *Journal of Political Power* 5, no. 1 (April 1, 2012): 137–152. doi: 10.1080/2158379X.2012.660026.

Lovett, Frank, and Philip Pettit. "Preserving Republican Freedom: A Reply to Simpson." *Philosophy & Public Affairs* 46, no. 4 (2018): 363–383. doi: 10.1111/papa.12126.

Luca, Michael, Deepak Malhotra, and Christopher Poliquin. "Handgun Waiting Periods Reduce Gun Deaths." *Proceedings of the National Academy of Sciences* 114, no. 46 (November 14, 2017): 12162–12165. doi: 10.1073/pnas.1619896114.

Ludwig, Jens. "Reducing Gun Violence in America." *Proceedings of the National Academy of Sciences* 114, no. 46 (November 14, 2017): 12097–12099. doi: 10.1073/pnas.1717306114.

Lund, Nelson. "The Future of the Second Amendment in a Time of Lawless Violence." SSRN Scholarly Paper. Rochester, NY, September 28, 2020. doi: 10.2139/ssrn.3701185.

Lynch, Kellie R., Tk Logan, and Dylan B. Jackson. "'People Will Bury Their Guns before They Surrender Them': Implementing Domestic Violence Gun Control in Rural, Appalachian versus Urban Communities: Appalachian Domestic Violence Gun Control." *Rural Sociology* 83, no. 2 (June 2018): 315–346. doi: 10.1111/ruso.12206.

Lyon, Peter. "This Is What Zero Tolerance For Drink Driving Looks Like." Forbes. Accessed March 6, 2023. https://www.forbes.com/sites/peterlyon/2020/08/27/frightening-consequences-for-drink-drivers-in-japan/.

Makowsky, Michael D., and Patrick L. Warren. "Firearms and Lynching." SSRN Scholarly Paper. Rochester, NY, August 7, 2022. doi: 10.2139/ssrn.3727462.

Martela, Joshua, and Frank Hicks. "A New Dimension to a Meaningful Life." *Scientific American.* Accessed September 28, 2022. https://www.scientificamerican.com/article/a-new-dimension-to-a-meaningful-life1/.

McCann, Anthony. *Shadowlands: Fear and Freedom at the Oregon Standoff.* 1st Edition. New York: Bloomsbury Publishing, 2019.

McConnell, Allen R. "The Multiple Self-Aspects Framework: Self-Concept Representation and Its Implications." *Personality and Social Psychology Review* 15, no. 1 (February 1, 2011): 3–27. doi: 10.1177/1088868310371101.

McMahan, Jeff. "Why Gun 'Control' Is Not Enough." Opinionator, 1355940232. https://archive.nytimes.com/opinionator.blogs.nytimes.com/2012/12/19/why-gun-control-is-not-enough/.

Mencken, F Carson, and Paul Froese. "Gun Culture in Action." *Social Problems* 66, no. 1 (February 1, 2019): 3–27. doi: 10.1093/socpro/spx040.

Metcalf, Thomas. "GUN VIOLENCE AS INDUSTRIAL POLLUTION," n.d., 41.

Monuteaux, Michael C., Lois K. Lee, David Hemenway, Rebekah Mannix, and Eric W. Fleegler. "Firearm Ownership and Violent Crime in the U.S." *American Journal of Preventive Medicine* 49, no. 2 (August 2015): 207–214. doi: 10.1016/j.amepre.2015.02.008.

Nagata, T., S. Setoguchi, D. Hemenway, and M. J. Perry. "Effectiveness of a Law to Reduce Alcohol-Impaired Driving in Japan." *Injury Prevention* 14, no. 1 (February 1, 2008): 19–23. doi: 10.1136/ip.2007.015719.

Nagin, Daniel S., Christopher S. Koper, and Cynthia Lum. "Policy Recommendations for Countering Mass Shootings in the United States." *Criminology & Public Policy* 19, no. 1 (February 2020): 9–15. doi: 10.1111/1745-9133.12484.

O'Neill, Martin. "What Should Egalitarians Believe?" *Philosophy & Public Affairs* 36, no. 2 (2008): 119–156. doi: 10.1111/j.1088-4963.2008.00130.x.

Orsi, Robert A. *History and Presence.* Reprint edition. Cambridge, MA and London: Belknap Press: An Imprint of Harvard University Press, 2018.

Patten, Alan. "Are The Economic Liberties Basic?" *Critical Review* 26, no. 3–4 (October 2, 2014): 362–374. doi: 10.1080/08913811.2014.947745.

Pecanha, Sergio. "Opinion | Lockdown Drills: An American Quirk, out of Control." *Washington Post.* Accessed September 27, 2022. https://www.washingtonpost.com/opinions/2019/10/11/lockdown-drills-an-american-quirk-out-control/.

Pettit, Philip. *On the People's Terms: A Republican Theory and Model of Democracy.* The Seeley Lectures. Cambridge: Cambridge University Press, 2012. doi: 10.1017/CBO9781139017428.

———. *Republicanism: A Theory of Freedom and Government*. 1st edition. Oxford and New York: Clarendon Press, 1997.

Platz, Jeppe von. "Are Economic Liberties Basic Rights?" *Politics, Philosophy & Economics* 13, no. 1 (February 1, 2014): 23–44. doi: 10.1177/1470594 X13483466.

Pogue, James. *Chosen Country: A Rebellion in the West*. New York: Henry Holt and Co., 2018.

PolitiFact. "Does Joe Biden's Plan Tax Semi-Automatic Firearms?" Accessed September 27, 2022. https://www.politifact.com/article/2020/nov/01/does-joe-bidens-plan-tax-semi-automatic-firearms/.

RAND Corporation. "What Science Tells Us About the Effects of Gun Policies," January 10, 2023. https://www.rand.org/research/gun-policy/key-findings/what-science-tells-us-about-the-effects-of-gun-policies.html.

Rawls, John. *A Theory of Justice*. Cambridge, MA: Harvard University Press, 2009.

———. *Political Liberalism*. Expanded edition. New York: Columbia University Press, 2005.

Remkus, Ashley. "We Spent A Year Investigating Police Dogs. Here Are Six Takeaways." The Marshall Project, October 2, 2020. https://www.themarshallproject.org/2020/10/02/we-spent-a-year-investigating-police-dogs-here-are-six-takeaways.

Robison, Jennifer. "Decades of Drug Use: Data From the '60s and '70s." Gallup.com, July 2, 2002. https://news.gallup.com/poll/6331/Decades-Drug-Use-Data-From-60s-70s.aspx.

Roman, Meredith. "The Black Panther Party and the Struggle for Human Rights." *Spectrum: A Journal on Black Men* 5, no. 1 (2016): 7–32. doi: 10.2979/spectrum.5.1.02.

Rose, Julie L. *Free Time*. Princeton, NJ and Oxford: Princeton University Press, 2016.

Rudolph, Kara E., Elizabeth A. Stuart, Jon S. Vernick, and Daniel W. Webster. "Association Between Connecticut's Permit-to-Purchase Handgun Law and Homicides." *American Journal of Public Health* 105, no. 8 (August 2015): e49–54. doi: 10.2105/AJPH.2015.302703.

Sandven, Hallvard. "Systemic Domination, Social Institutions and the Coalition Problem." *Politics, Philosophy & Economics* 19, no. 4 (November 2020): 382–402. doi: 10.1177/1470594X20927927.

Santaella-Tenorio, Julian, Magdalena Cerdá, Andrés Villaveces, and Sandro Galea. "What Do We Know About the Association Between Firearm Legislation and Firearm-Related Injuries?" *Epidemiologic Reviews* 38, no. 1 (January 1, 2016): 140–157. doi: 10.1093/epirev/mxv012.

Scheffler, Samuel. *Equality and Tradition: Questions of Value in Moral and Political Theory.* 1st edition. New York and Oxford: Oxford University Press, 2012.

Schell, Terry L., Matthew Cefalu, Beth Ann Griffin, Rosanna Smart, and Andrew R. Morral. "Changes in Firearm Mortality Following the Implementation of State Laws Regulating Firearm Access and Use." *Proceedings of the National Academy of Sciences* 117, no. 26 (June 30, 2020): 14906–14910. doi: 10.1073/pnas.1921965117.

Schmidt, Andreas T. "Domination without Inequality? Mutual Domination, Republicanism, and Gun Control." *Philosophy & Public Affairs* 46, no. 2 (April 2018): 175–206. doi: 10.1111/papa.12119.

Schuppe, Jon. "America's Rifle: Why so Many People Love the AR-15." Accessed September 27, 2022. https://www.nbcnews.com/news/us-news/america-s-rifle-why-so-many-people-love-ar-15-n831171.

Schwartz, Joanna. "The Case Against Qualified Immunity." *Notre Dame Law Review* 93, no. 5 (August 1, 2018): 1797.

Setiya, Kieran. "Ignorance, Beneficence, and Rights." *Journal of Moral Philosophy* 17, no. 1 (February 19, 2020): 56–74. doi: 10.1163/17455243–20182841.

Shapshay, Sandra. "A Two-Tiered Theory of the Sublime." *The British Journal of Aesthetics* 61, no. 2 (April 1, 2021): 123–143. doi: 10.1093/aesthj/ayaa047.

——. "At Once Tiny and Huge: How Philosophers Describe the Feeling We Call 'Sublime.'" Text. Scroll.in. https://scroll.in. Accessed September 28, 2022. https://scroll.in/article/904615/at-once-tiny-and-huge-how-philosophers-describe-the-feeling-we-call-sublime.

Sher, Heather. "What I Saw Treating the Victims From Parkland Should Change the Debate on Guns." *The Atlantic*, February 22, 2018. https://www.theatlantic.com/politics/archive/2018/02/what-i-saw-treating-the-victims-from-parkland-should-change-the-debate-on-guns/553937/.

Shermer, Michael. "Opinion | Guns Aren't a Bulwark Against Tyranny. The Rule of Law Is." *The New York Times*, October 5, 2017, sec. Opinion. https://www.nytimes.com/2017/10/05/opinion/gun-rights-vegas-massacre.html.

Shiffrin, Seana Valentine. "Promising, Intimate Relationships, and Conventionalism." *The Philosophical Review* 117, no. 4 (October 1, 2008): 481–524. doi: 10.1215/00318108-2008-014.

Siegel, Michael. "Implications of the Australian Experience With Firearm Regulation for US Gun Policy." *American Journal of Public Health* 108, no. 11 (November 2018): 1438–1439. doi: 10.2105/AJPH.2018.304720.

Siegel, Michael, Max Goder-Reiser, Grant Duwe, Michael Rocque, James Alan Fox, and Emma E. Fridel. "The Relation between State Gun Laws and the Incidence and Severity of Mass Public Shootings in the United States, 1976–2018." *Law and Human Behavior* 44, no. 5 (October 2020): 347–360. doi: 10.1037/lhb0000378.

Siegel, Michael, Ziming Xuan, Craig S. Ross, Sandro Galea, Bindu Kalesan, Eric Fleegler, and Kristin A. Goss. "Easiness of Legal Access to Concealed Firearm Permits and Homicide Rates in the United States." *American Journal of Public Health* 107, no. 12 (December 2017): 1923–1929. doi: 10.2105/AJPH.2017.304057.

Simas, Elizabeth N., Scott Clifford, and Justin H. Kirkland. "How Empathic Concern Fuels Political Polarization." *American Political Science Review* 114, no. 1 (February 2020): 258–269. doi: 10.1017/S0003055419000534.

Simpson, Thomas W. "The Impossibility of Republican Freedom." *Philosophy & Public Affairs* 45, no. 1 (2017): 27–53. doi: 10.1111/papa.12082.

Smith, Michael R., and Matthew Petrocelli. "The Effect of Concealed Handgun Carry Deregulation in Arizona on Crime in Tucson." *Criminal Justice Policy Review* 30, no. 8 (October 2019): 1186–1203. doi: 10.1177/0887403418782739.

Smith, Victoria M., Michael Siegel, Ziming Xuan, Craig S. Ross, Sandro Galea, Bindu Kalesan, Eric Fleegler, and Kristin A. Goss. "Broadening the Perspective on Gun Violence: An Examination of the Firearms Industry, 1990–2015." *American Journal of Preventive Medicine* 53, no. 5 (November 2017): 584–591. doi: 10.1016/j.amepre.2017.05.002.

Soss, Joe, and Vesla Weaver. "Police Are Our Government: Politics, Political Science, and the Policing of Race–Class Subjugated Communities." *Annual Review of Political Science* 20, no. 1 (2017): 565–591. doi: 10.1146/annurev-polisci-060415-093825.

Spross, Jeff. "How Obama Diagnosed Trumpism Way Back in 2008." *The Week*. Accessed August 28, 2022. https://theweek.com/articles/610945/how-obama-diagnosed-trumpism-way-back-2008.

Strain, Christopher B. *Pure Fire: Self-Defense as Activism in the Civil Rights Era*. Athens, GA: University of Georgia Press, 2005.

Street, Joe. *The Culture War in the Civil Rights Movement*. 1st edition. Gainesville, FL: University Press of Florida, 2007.

Sunstein, Cass R. "Sludge Audits." *Behavioural Public Policy*, January 6, 2020, 1–20. doi: 10.1017/bpp.2019.32.

Suprenant, Chris. "Minority Oppression and Justified Revolution." Accessed October 1, 2022. https://onlinelibrary.wiley.com/doi/abs/10.1111/j.1467-9833.2010.01509.x.

Sutton, Joe, "Harvey Updyke, Who Poisoned Iconic Oak Trees at Auburn, Dies at 71." CNN, July 31, 2020. Accessed February 14, 2023. https://www.cnn.com/2020/07/31/us/harvey-updyke-alabama-auburn-dead/index.html.

Taylor, Benjamin, and Jing Li. "Do Fewer Guns Lead to Less Crime? Evidence from Australia." *International Review of Law and Economics* 42 (June 2015): 72–78. doi: 10.1016/j.irle.2015.01.002.

Tomasi, John. *Free Market Fairness*. Princeton, NJ: Princeton University Press, 2012. doi: 10.1515/9781400842391.

Towers, Sherry, Danielle Wallace, and David Hemenway. "Temporal Trends in Public Mass Shootings: High-Capacity Magazines Significantly Increase Fatality Counts, and Are Becoming More Prevalent." Preprint. *Public and Global Health*, December 15, 2019. doi: 10.1101/2019.12.12.19014738.

"United States v. Bundy, 968 F.3d 1019 | Casetext Search + Citator." Accessed October 10, 2022. https://casetext.com/case/united-states-v-bundy-95.

Vars, Frederick, and Ian Ayres. "Suicide Accounts for Most Gun Deaths. A Libertarian Approach Could Help. - WSJ." Accessed September 27, 2022. https://www.wsj.com/articles/suicide-accounts-for-most-gun-deaths-a-libertarian-approach-could-help-11602717798.

Vars, Fredrick E., and Angela Selvaggio. "'Bind Me More Tightly Still': Voluntary Restraint Against Gun Suicide." SSRN Scholarly Paper. Rochester, NY, August 7, 2015. doi: 10.2139/ssrn.2641139.

Wallace, Lacey N. "Concealed Ownership: Americans' Perceived Comfort Sharing Gun Ownership Status with Others." *Sociological Spectrum* 37, no. 5 (September 3, 2017): 267–281. doi: 10.1080/02732173.2017.1348278.

Weaver, Vesla M., and Gwen Prowse. "Racial Authoritarianism in U.S. Democracy." *Science* 369, no. 6508 (September 4, 2020): 1176–1178. doi: 10.1126/science.abd7669.

Weaver, Vesla, Gwen Prowse, and Spencer Piston. "Too Much Knowledge, Too Little Power: An Assessment of Political Knowledge in Highly Policed Communities." *The Journal of Politics* 81, no. 3 (July 2019): 1153–1166. doi: 10.1086/703538.

Webster, Daniel W., Alexander D. McCourt, Cassandra K. Crifasi, Marisa D. Booty, and Elizabeth A. Stuart. "Evidence Concerning the Regulation of Firearms Design, Sale, and Carrying on Fatal Mass Shootings in the United States." *Criminology & Public Policy* 19, no. 1 (February 2020): 171–212. doi: 10.1111/1745–9133.12487.

Wellman, Christopher Heath. *Rights Forfeiture and Punishment.* Oxford: Oxford University Press, 2017.

Welna, David. "Democrats Call For Anonymous Policing Of Protests To End." *NPR*, June 4, 2020. https://www.npr.org/2020/06/04/870048760/no-names-no-insignias-democrats-call-for-anonymous-policing-of-protests-to-end.

Wendt, Simon. "Protection or Path Toward Revolution?: Black Power and Self-Defense." *Souls* 9, no. 4 (December 6, 2007): 320–332. doi: 10.1080/10999940701703778.

———. *The Spirit and the Shotgun: Armed Resistance and the Struggle for Civil Rights.* 1st edition. Gainesville, FL: University Press of Florida, 2007.

———. "'They Finally Found Out That We Really Are Men': Violence, Non-Violence and Black Manhood in the Civil Rights Era." *Gender & History* 19, no. 3 (2007): 543–564. doi: 10.1111/j.1468–0424.2007.00487.x.

Westlund, Andrea C. "Selflessness and Responsibility for Self: Is Deference Compatible with Autonomy?" *The Philosophical Review* 112, no. 4 (2003): 483–523.

Wiles, Tay. "How the Feds Helped Make Cliven Bundy a Celebrity." *High Country News*, April 30, 2018. https://www.hcn.org/issues/50.7/sagebrush-rebellion-celebrity-scofflaw.

Williams, David. "Civic Republicanism and the Citizen Militia: The Terrifying Second Amendment." *Yale Law Journal*, January 1, 1991. https://openyls.law.yale.edu/handle/20.500.13051/8675.

Wintemute, Garen J. "Background Checks For Firearm Purchases: Problem Areas And Recommendations To Improve Effectiveness." *Health Affairs* 38, no. 10 (October 1, 2019): 1702–1710. doi: 10.1377/hlthaff. 2019.00671.

Zhao, Huanhuan, Heyun Zhang, Yan Xu, Jiamei Lu, and Wen He. "Relation Between Awe and Environmentalism: The Role of Social Dominance Orientation." *Frontiers in Psychology* 9 (2018). https://www.frontiersin. org/articles/10.3389/fpsyg.2018.02367.

For Product Safety Concerns and Information please contact our EU
representative GPSR@taylorandfrancis.com
Taylor & Francis Verlag GmbH, Kaufingerstraße 24, 80331 München, Germany

* 9 7 8 0 3 6 7 1 4 1 0 7 3 *